Also by the Authors

Emma Mactaggart B.Bus (Mkting)

Picture Books
I Can Do Anything
Lily Fabourama Glamourama
Imagine If... (expected release date: Nov 2012)

Memoirs
Eggs Contradict
Interpersonal Relations
The Little Black Cookbook

Boogie Books Published
A Child's View, An Anthology

Ainsley Shepherd B.Bus/Arts (Mkting, PR, Comm)

Picture Books
Slow Down Sarah (expected release date: Nov 2012)

childwrites

Creating a Children's Picture Book is Child's Play

First published 2012 by Boogie Books in Australia
Text © Emma Mactaggart
Text © Ainsley Shepherd
Illustrations © Emma Mactaggart
Stick Figure Illustrations © Georgia Mactaggart

National Library of Australia
Cataloguing-in-Publication data:

Mactaggart, Emma 1969 -
Shepherd, Ainsley 1977 -

Child Writes
Creating a Children's Picture Book is Child's Play
A step-by-step guide to writing and illustrating a children's picture book.
by Emma Mactaggart; edited by Ainsley Shepherd.

Edition: 1st ed
ISBN: 9781921926006 (pbk)
Series: Child Writes.
Subjects: Children's literature--Authorship.
Children's literature--Illustrations.

Other Authors/Contributors: Shepherd, Ainsley.

Dewey Number: 808.068

Designed by bcreative, Michelle Von Pein

Printed in China through Red Planet Print Management

boogie
books
helping children understand their world
www.boogiebooks.com.au

child
writes

Creating a Children's Picture Book is Child's Play

A step-by-step guide to writing and illustrating
a children's picture book

Written by Emma Mactaggart
Edited by Ainsley Shepherd

By Way of **Introduction**

The creative process – regardless of whether the platform is music, literature, dance or visual arts – is an intensely satisfying one, which can be peppered with frustration and limitations!

Creative endeavours are the outpourings of those who are passionate about what they do. For anyone embarking upon the journey of learning within any of these endeavours, there is a plethora of advice proffered by these same passionate practitioners, who are often only one step ahead.

We would love to tell you that the creation of a children's picture book is a quick and easy process. In reality, it is not quick and easy, but it is a process. And it is possible. At the end of the day, the reward you will experience when you hold your published children's picture book in your hands cannot easily be surpassed. This is regardless of your motivation for writing in the first place – whether you are intending to give a gift of words and images in book form (much like the gift of a labour of love, like a quilt), or write the next bestseller in the children's picture book market.

To make the process more manageable, we have intentionally broken it down into clear steps. And we've been incredibly honest and revealed the potential pitfalls, so that you can avoid them. We recommend that you first of all read the whole book through, so that you can get the big picture of the process it entails. Then go back and follow the plan we've laid out, step-by-step.

The methodology in this guide has been tested since 2004 and children between the ages of nine and twelve have been the students. We know it works.

If a child can do it, why can't you?

We're excited to walk step-by-step with you, to help you turn your dream into reality. Enjoy the journey!

Thank you.

Emma and Ainsley

Foreword by Annie O'Dowd

Creativity is sometimes like magic. To make a lovely work of art or construct a perfect sentence can not only be immensely satisfying, but bring the maker a sense of mastery and order. From out of the ordinary, beauty is moulded; from chaos, an exciting set of ideas is brought forth. But the artist does not always control his or her abilities. The process of bringing to birth what lies hidden can be difficult. At times our muse seems to have vanished and we are stranded, unable to express ourselves. Then, suddenly, like a dam breaking, our connection returns, rushes out and we race to keep up with the tumble of ideas that seem to flow effortlessly with perfect clarity. Perhaps this is why creative powers are sometimes viewed with reverence. Harnessing creativity in both ourselves and others is a gift. Teachers can guide us but we too can learn strategies to tap the source and bring forth what is already there in abundance.

Creativity is not only the precinct of the talented or the 'artistic' soul. It is universal. Being alive is creative. Creativity is our birthright. One only has to watch a small child at play to witness this in miniature. Children delight us with their antics as they dress up, take on roles and make up little stories that, like a stream of consciousness, are funny, touching, and often a nonsensical soup of their experiences. Little children use creative play to make sense of their world; to take charge of it. When we are adult, we have a much more complex relationship with our creative selves. In part, we are hampered by knowledge and experience yet it is these very things that feed and give structure to our endeavours.

In this sense, we are all potential artists, writers and actors. Each of us has within us the life force which connects us not only with each other through unseen currents but, even with the sacred. Whether or not you believe in a force greater than yourself, in creating we mimic the divine. Of course we also need skills to make it happen, but in order to tap into that special dimension we need the unnamable... the wisp of smoke that is inspiration. Only in seeking this delicate opening can we find the connection that will transmute our ideas into that ancient and magic currency – stories.

Stories too, are universal; an oral tradition stretching back to our earliest beginnings. Stories existed before written language and perhaps even before any other kind of human culture. They bind us together, teach us, help us to share experience and express who we are. Stories are multi-layered. On the surface they transport us to other places and seize us in the grip of plot and character but underneath, stories hold more subtle layers of meaning, helping us to understand the experience of being human.

Naturally, inspiration is not the only thread in the creative process. Once we have begun work on an idea that 'takes', there is a long struggle before us. Most of what we need to complete our project is made of humbler clay: persistence, perspiration and confidence. Self-belief will buoy you up when your inspiration falters and persistence will push you onwards when you lose faith, but pure hard work is what gets you there in the long run. Somebody once said that nothing worthwhile is easily achieved and this is definitely true of any creative aspiration. But don't let this dampen your spirits, only remember that as you struggle towards perfection, it is normal to feel discouraged many times before you reach your goal.

For children, to be able to create their own books is a richly rewarding experience. It will help them to shape their ideas and build their confidence, and teach them about words, colour, texture and design. The benefit to be gleaned from the arc of the creative process is far reaching for both teacher and student. The beautiful little covers, featured at the end of each chapter, along with the quotes submitted by the children from the Child Writes program, are truly amazing. I found myself wanting to turn the covers and see what they had created. The designs of the covers themselves are so many and varied, it is easy to see the care that has been taken with every choice of colour, illustration and title. For anyone, regardless of age or experience, who has the burning desire to bring their ideas into being, 'Child Writes' is a rich source of encouragement, guidance and simple step-by-step instructions. Emma Mactaggart's enthusiasm for the entire process is apparent from the very first paragraph and her tireless investigation of every possible detail, leaves the budding author inspired!

Table of Contents

Preface

You have a burning desire to create something or to teach others to create something... I know! Otherwise you wouldn't have bought this book.

YOU are exactly the person I wrote this for.

I can just imagine your search for a step-by-step resource guide which takes you through the ENTIRE writing, illustrating and publishing process; beginning with extracting an idea from your head and ending with you reading your words on pages which may even be decorated by your beautiful illustrations. But to reach that point, you knew you needed to understand how to organise the printing, the promotion and indeed, all the other practical jobs and responsibilities which fall to an individual along the exciting and self-fulfilling journey which is creating a children's picture book.

How do my words fit a children's picture book format? How do I plan and design a double spread? How do I contact a library? Who can I contact for assistance? How much time will it take? Will I make any money? Who organises an ISBN? How do I price my book? There can be thousands of questions to ask, each requiring an answer. All of a sudden, the entire process can look too daunting and overwhelming. Sometimes it feels as though it would be easier to just forget it.

I would seriously suggest putting all questions aside for a moment, and trust me as I lead you through the step-by-step process – a journey which you can not only complete, but also enjoy.

Even though you have already purchased this book, I should establish my credentials before you turn another page. After all, I really want you to take everything I give you and RUN WITH IT.

I am an accidental author – at least this is what I tell children as I introduce myself, when I speak to groups at schools. I was a mad keen letter writer when I was younger and I seriously enjoyed it when a recipient would say to me "Ah, your letter made me cry", or "It made me laugh". There is something intrinsically satisfying in affecting people through words. This – combined with a nearly nauseating passion for sharing anything I am interested in – is why I write.

In a past life, I have worked in partnership with a friend in a catering business, traded admin support time in a gallery for art class time and worked innumerable shifts in a hardware store. I have sat in train carriages as a tourism assistant, prepared marketing plans for scaffolders, and worked my way through TAFE and uni (working in bars, selling roses, telemarketing, waitressing, painting, tiling...). Now I am filling my days with even more traditional work – being a mother to three children. I believe the latter job is HARDER than anything associated with a secretarial course, a business degree and parts thereof of a visual arts certificate!

I suspect I am very much like you and have discovered (amidst my eclectic day to day lifestyle) that I have a penchant for writing and for sharing. Having a full and rewarding world is a wonderful point of entry for any writer, with so much to experience to draw upon. It can be a hindrance as well, as you juggle the many responsibilities you already have.

Of course, it is what I have been doing for the past couple of years specifically which will be of interest to you. Back to the 'accidental author' bit... I wrote a lovely list of 'empowering' thoughts for my second daughter in 2003. She loved it! I added more and more words. When she started to lose interest, I drew some pictures – and she was interested again, and so were her friends. I pretended to be a graphic designer and set it up as 'book' and pressed *print* on the photocopier. With a sprinkle of colour, a dash of love and a dose of optimism, I investigated the options of printing it 'properly'. It all seemed manageable – especially when I fiddled with the numbers and realised if I sold so many, I would break even, and if I kept selling more copies I WOULD BE LOADED! I drove the printers nuts until they rang and said my first order of 1,000 children's picture books was ready.

Have you any idea, any at all, how much space 1,000 books takes up? We are only talking about twenty-six pages of book, A4 size. It was ridiculous! I nearly blew a tyre on the way home! The boxes were packed in around my children, they filled the boot beyond capacity, and they were extremely heavy... well, the last ones certainly weighed more than the first ones! My kids sat in the doorway of the house as one by one, I lugged the boxes from the car, lined them up in the garage and with a sweaty brow and a 'Right, that job's done!', I turned on my heel and swept them up, and we went inside to continue on with a very normal home day. It was not until the two little ones tried to get back into the car to pick up the first-born beauty from school, that I realised we couldn't even open the doors to the car! So I reversed out, cursing my optimism, and for the first time had a few second thoughts.

Now it was time to be methodical. Slowly and surely, I sold those books, wrote and illustrated another one the next year (2,000 copies!) and did the same. With optimism, I embarked on book number three the following year. One book a year, surely that was not so ambitious? I had a business name, I had purchased a list of ISBNs, I had sold nearly 3,000 copies, and I had plans!

I was interrupted by my gorgeous girls as I dragged out the drawing table. They had held a meeting. I was impressed – they were only seven, five and three!

"Please Mummy, please don't do another book. It takes you away from us."

Now, I have listened at seminars, workshops and festivals about incredible women who manage to work successfully for years with children at their feet, producing enough income to keep everyone afloat and who still have close relationships with those children. I didn't have enough faith in myself. After all, I am the type of person who gets so distracted by anything that I will inevitably burn the potatoes. I was already operating at full tote, so to speak, and I had to concede to my children!

So, what do you do? I really wanted to keep going. Short stories, visual diaries, notebooks – all became my companions. Even now around my office as I type, I have pages of writing, half-baked stories, colourful images, thoughts and contemplations. I did win a place in an anthology for a short story. I have helped friends produce their own books. I have a number of children's picture books in various stages surrounding me.

All along, I have had the opportunity to be the grown-up writer. Whilst I was selling my books, I offered and accepted any offer to do 'author' visits to school or talks to librarians, or readings – ANYTHING. And no, I didn't charge any fees. There is something particularly attractive about someone who offers something for nothing! Each and every time, the introduction would be from someone I knew, like another parent with children at another school who would say, "Oh, will you talk at my school?" and I would say "Yes" to every invitation.

There were two amazing gigs which channelled me in the direction I am still following. The first was being invited by Jill Temple to be a Literacy Hero at Middle Ridge State School. (I was so nervous! I think they felt sorry for me.) Jill is a generous, creative sage, and when she starts a conversation with "I've been thinking you should...", you know to listen! The second was a workshop with librarians at a district seminar. (I spoke, still nervous as anything and making up the workshop as I went. Then, I *knew* they felt sorry for me!) There I met Jan Watkins. Jan became my 'agent' and had me travelling around the city and the surrounding district for book weeks, year after year, doing author talks, which allowed me to hone my presentation skills.

The following year, I finished the USQ McGregor Summer School's Illustrations Course with Rebecca Berrett. With seventy hours of contact time, we learnt the entire process of illustrating a picture book and exhibited an example of what publishers are looking for in a dummy rough. Now I had written two books and now I knew how to illustrate a book properly, as opposed to illustrating instinctively! If I couldn't work on another book myself, surely I could show others how to do it.

Sometimes, it simply pays to say your thoughts aloud. A conversation with Jill about the plethora of courses which are available to adults, and yet nothing for children. As I write it now, I can't believe how harmless this sounds – doesn't it?!

The soon-to-be-named Child Writes workshop started as a six hour journey with a group of children. The goal was to create a character, or a setting, or a plot - to arm the children with at least one of these vital elements – and then shoot through! The thing was, the children became enraptured by the process and we could see magical stories unfolding right in front of our eyes. Fortunately the school didn't require any prompting. Indeed, the staff at the school focused on building my confidence to keep going. And we did just that – kept going!

The 'guts' of the books were produced using an office photocopier and the covers were printed using the last remnants of cash from the petty cash tin. There was a book launch, the purchase of an ISBN and the books were bundled up and copies sent to the National and Queensland State Library. The children had become published authors, and I had become a teacher and a publisher! To say the process was immensely rewarding and satisfying and brilliantly wonderful is an excessive understatement.

Child Writes was born… I just didn't know it yet!

Teaching children to write and illustrate their own picture books became my focus. I could fit it in when my children were at school, and they didn't notice I was folding clothes late into the night, or packing lunch boxes as the sun faintly began to share its celebration of a new day. They also didn't care their uniforms may have missed being ironed, their vegemite sandwiches were a little squishy or that their sheets may not have been changed as often. They had their wish and I had mine.

This same fabulous school asked me if I was interested in coming back the following year. It wasn't a difficult decision. OF COURSE! I could do this!

Now I have talked and taught and edited and designed and published the works of well over two hundred children who have written and illustrated their own picture books. And the most magical part is that the children each donated a copy of their book to the children's ward at the local hospital. This gave them a sense of purpose. The books also offer incredible motivation to the children who read those books in the middle of the night, when the wards are quiet and their parents have gone home, when they see what a peer can achieve.

It is wonderful when a project you embrace begins to unfold in front of you – especially one which is led by instinctive responses and is supported by the generosity of those around you. The process of writing to share is marvellous! The thought of a gift being generated by you for another person is completely gratifying.

Imagine how every one of those children felt at Christmas time as they gave a book they had written and illustrated to their parent, grandparent, sibling or friend. Some people indulge in giving as they share their cooking; gift a quilt; create a painting, a drawing, a piece of decoupage, a photo scrapbook; or give time teaching others about their passion.

I write.

It doesn't get any better... and now it is your turn.

x

Emma

PS Just so you know, in the 'In the Words of a Child' section at the end of each chapter, these thoughts and musings are from children who have been through the Child Writes process and are now published authors.

| Imagine it

It all starts with an idea.

Now, you can skip this bit if you surfaced this morning with a clear picture of a wonderful story for children in your mind's eye – if you can see your main character, a setting which wraps around the character like a second skin and you know exactly what is going to happen in the beginning, the middle and at the end of the story.

If it is kind of like pressing 'Play' and watching a movie, you may want to forge right ahead.

But, if you are not entirely sure what you are writing about, yet you have already envisaged the delight on the first recipients face – keep reading!

A staggering number of ideas are already in your head right now. Literally, right now! All you need to do is shut down all the other functions your body has to contend with, and allow time to focus on what is in your head. You have already consumed the sights and sounds which will become a character, a setting, or a plot. You have already had the thoughts, the feelings, and the experiences which will make your story believable.

Every one of us is capable of producing hundreds, if not thousands, of ideas over our lifetime. Given a pen and paper and a propensity to share the idea – *voilà*! You have the beginning of a story.

I have been working with children, teaching them how to write and illustrate their own picture books. What is so inspiring is that children are so relaxed about the process of creating a story and they simply need to be steered in the right direction. Think of it. We tell each other stories every day – stories about ourselves, our work and our adventures. We are already experienced without even realising it!

Story writing itself is simply layering – one layer at a time reflecting each part of the process; from the generation of an idea, the actual work of getting words onto paper, the multiple layers of editing and finally the end product.

Be warned, however: all along the way, you may experience discomfort. You may well be thinking, 'What a risky statement to include in the beginning of a book she wants us to read in its entirety!' I guess the truth of the matter is that often, when we experience this discomfort, or doubt, or lack of will, it is usually because we are lacking the confidence to push through this micro-pain barrier. The belief that you are capable of attempting things for the first time is called self-efficacy. If you have a high level of self-efficacy, you strongly believe you have the capability to pursue a set of actions which will ensure you reach your goal. If you have a low level of self-efficacy, you will probably give up, because you don't really believe you are capable of taking the steps to reach the end goal.

I mention this now, because each page from now on is to serve as a 'hand holder'. And if you for a second doubt you are capable of producing your own children's picture book, then I am right here to remind you that YOU CAN!

As soon as you doubt yourself, just do the tasks set out in front of you and you will find you have accomplished another step on the way to the end goal.

Anthony Gunn is a guru of fear management and translates self-efficacy into manageable exercises in his book, **Raising Confident, Happy Children**. It certainly will help you understand yourself if you read it (even if you have a handle on your own self-efficacy). In addition, by identifying areas which require support for your children's development, you may even find a raft of wonderful story ideas!

Before you start though, look around you. Is your working environment inspiring? Are you comfortable enough to sit there now for hour after hour? Do you need to be away from your home, your desk? Do you need good light, music, or to kick off your shoes? Whatever you need physically around you, it is important to be very comfortable.

Get into the Right Frame of Mind
Breathe

As I said earlier, all the ideas you may have are there – locked up inside your head! It is a matter of releasing the creativity which lurks within. Everything you have ever heard, seen, experienced or learned is already there, in your head. You just need to extract it. And the first step is to relax. There is nothing worse than being given a blank piece of paper with a tight timeframe and being told to just write... so, let's breathe.

Breathe? Yes, breathe!

Close your eyes. Use your finger to press down on one side of your nose and breathe in, listening to the sound of the air moving through your head. As you exhale, press the other side. Keep alternating, deep breaths, until you feel very relaxed. It is a simple exercise, which I use to start each and EVERY writing session myself. It will serve to accomplish a few things for you. Firstly, a foreign exercise may make you feel uncomfortable, and that's good because we often feel uncomfortable in the process of writing, illustrating or sharing, and we need to get used to it. Additionally, it serves as a circuit-breaker – a way to distinguish there is a change in the order of the day, and you are no longer a student or a worker, mother, father etc. Rather, you are now a writer and an illustrator. Finally, it allows you to relax, and relaxing is the BEST way to allow for the flow of ideas.

Draw
Contour Drawing

Pick up a pencil in the OPPOSITE hand to the one you usually use. Hold a piece of paper firmly with your writing hand and now, looking at any object in front of you, start 'tracing' it with your eyes. Move the hand holding the pencil to mimic your eye movements. This actually has a name! It is called contour drawing. You are recording on paper the lines (or contours) which make an object recognisable to the viewer.

Blind Contour Drawing

Now, you need to really push yourself and try to draw WITHOUT looking at the paper at all. Rather, you are going to look at the object 100 per cent of the time. You are 'blind' to the paper and you can only 'see' the object.

This exercise comes with a warning, though. You may find your drawings too funny to bear and you may end up laughing! Or, you will probably look at the drawing and think it too stupid to continue. To ensure you don't throw this book out the window right now, please remember that you are not trying to actually draw an object for a viewer. The aim is to connect your hand with your eyes.

Once you have conquered this, try again with your usual writing hand and you will be amazed at the outcome.

Blind Contour Drawing: Hand

In this excercise, your hand is the object. Mean, aren't I?! For many people, hands are one of the most loathed parts of the body when it comes to drawing.

A SIDE THOUGHT...

Right Brain vs. Left Brain:

A great deal of study was conducted in the late '60s regarding the function of the brain. In response to the findings of the day, **Drawing on the Right Side of the Brain** drawing methods were developed by Betty Edwards in the late 1960s and early '70s. These methods were immortalised in this bestselling book, published in 1979. Since then, Dr Edwards' drawing methods have been used all over the world to teach millions of people how to draw.

In the classroom, we often discuss the roles of the right side of the brain vs. the left. Basically, the left-hand side is responsible for being analytical and seeing parts of the whole. Think of the stiff, angular lines which make up the letter *L*. It is responsible for us using phrases like 'That doesn't look correct', or working through a formula in a maths test.

The right-hand side is the creative side which allows us to draw what we see, making it easier to think about shapes and where an object (or part of an object) is in relation to something else. There is a fabulous exercise on the website (link below) and you can actually experience first-hand the 'click' you feel when you successfully move from the left-hand side of your brain to drawing with your right-hand side. Have a go! **www.drawright.com**

- Glance at the clock, so that you can time yourself. You want to know how long you can concentrate and draw without looking at the paper or away from the object.
- Anchor the piece of paper in front of you on the desk with a piece of tape.
- Hold the pencil in your writing hand.
- Use your opposite hand as the model.
- Do not lift the pencil from the page, making it a continuous line drawing.
- DO NOT LOOK AT THE PAPER AT ALL.

The premise behind this exercise is to help you improve your hand-eye communication. Again, you need to pretend the pencil is attached to your eyeball. Wherever your eye moves, it makes a 'mark' via your pencil.

It is an extraordinary truth that it is the ability of an artist to translate WHAT they see in front of them into some form of permanent medium, like paper or a canvas – rather than what they THINK they see. The Honourable Professor Lord Robert Winston actually recorded the eye movements of an artist for his award-winning BBC television series, '*The Human Body*'. The artist spends the majority of his time looking at the subject. When Lord Winston attempted to produce the same image (a portrait), he looked at *the canvas* the majority of the time.

You are certainly now in the right space to be creative. There a lots of wonderful ways to stimulate this creativity, and you may use one or all of these idea-source exercises.

The Ideas Toolbox
Idea Source: Doodle Drawing

This is the first of many idea-creating tools which we will explore. It may actually help you to create a character. For those of us who remember Mr Squiggle and his ability to extract yet another image from a few seemingly innocuous marks, this exercise is self-explanatory (of course, when I mention the guru of images, the children look at me as though I have gone quite mad).

For those of you not familiar with Mr Squiggle, start with a blank piece of paper.

On the paper, make one or more quick marks with your pencil. Within these marks is a something! It is a bit like looking at clouds as they pass and 'seeing' images within the formation.

What can you see? Rotate the paper around if you need to. Once you have 'discovered' something, then go over the lines you would like to embellish and add the extra lines you need, to develop your character. Simply ignore the lines you don't need for the moment. Don't rub them out.

As the character 'emerges', use all your drawing tools (cross-hatching, shading etc…) to give it more form and to indicate the light source. Now, start including more information, for example, the background.

Quickly make some written notes on the edge of the page if you have had a 'flash' of an idea about a story which may belong to the character.

Idea Source: Frankenstein

Don't worry, we are not going to mimic Victor Frankenstein (created by Mary Shelley in 1818) and head off to the butcher shops and dissecting rooms in order to source body parts to create a creature. Rather, the concept of construction from disparate parts gives rise to the opportunity to create a truly unique being, using just words.

I was first exposed to this exercise by James Moloney. I fortunately went to the wrong room – I had booked into an illustrator's workshop and ended up in a professional development workshop listening to James talking to a group of educators about how to teach the construction of a story to children! With a predetermined list of possible attributes, James encouraged us to 'create' our own character.

A SIDE THOUGHT...
The Attributes of a Writer or Illustrator:

Recently, I sat in a lecture theatre and listened with bated breath to a well-known author discuss exactly this. She believes you have to be born a writer or born an illustrator, and unless you are that person, give up. Well, that is a thought, but what if you didn't know you were born with these skills? I really believe all of us are born as storytellers and all of us are born capable of drawing.

After a brainstorming session with children, we decided that a writer and/or an illustrator is simply someone who is happy to share their thoughts! Some organise these thoughts in such a way as to be transferred via a mechanism we know as books. Others use mediums like magazines and more recently, web-associated mediums like blogs, twitter, Facebook, newsletters and online website diaries.

What do you need, then? Other than the desire to share, you need some paper and a pencil (or a computer and a keyboard). Even better, invest in a visual diary which can be your workbook, your recording mechanism for your story drafts, and it will become the beginning of a reference file. Everything you need!

Create a Human Character

1. Construct your own prompt-list of generic physical attributes belonging to a human (hair colour, skin tone, mouth shape, eye colour, teeth, age, gender, clothes, etc).
2. Put the list away for a while, because chances are you will already be formulating a character in your mind's eye.
3. After some time, take out the list. Do not think. I mean it! Take ten deep breaths and just do not think. Just respond to the list as quickly as possible.
4. There, it's as easy as that! In front of you – using words not lines – you have created a character. Now, if you are feeling very brave, draw the character!

Create a Non-Human Character

When I teach, I write the list and give the children choices from which they select one each (it is faster than those little hands writing, writing, writing).

See over the page for a short list as an example. Select one characteristic from each and *voilà* – a creature is born.

- Covering the body: feather, fur or scale?
- Extremities of limbs: talons, nails or claws?
- Shape of extremities: arm, limb, fin or wing?
- Mouth: fangs (razor-like or pointed?), tongue or teeth?

Now, with this written list in front of you, draw what you have in your mind's eye.

Again, as we did with the doodle drawing, give yourself a five-minute window to write some notes down which may yield a possible story.

> In that session with James Moloney, my answers for my character were banal at best! However, when the teacher beside me read out her responses, I began to see a character and instantly, I thought of a setting and a plot in which she would thrive – a Young Adult manuscript in the making.

You can also work with the same process, different parts coming together, using drawing not words. It is fun to 'answer' the above questions with a pencil rather than a pen.

Idea Source: Brainstorming

A brainstorm is defined as a 'brief psychological disturbance'. Brainstorming is 'to think quickly and creatively, to have an intensive group discussion in order to generate creative ideas and usually stimulate problem solving.' So, this is more fun if you are with a group of people.

The success of brainstorming relies on instinctive replies to a question. For example, if I say "Red" you may straight away answer "Stop" or "Lady Beetle". Record the first thing or things that come to mind. It is also really much more fun if you do this in a group.

Step One

Appoint a scribe. It is useful to have someone in front of the group, recording the responses.

Step Two

Start with the stimuli. For example, in our brainstorming sessions, we write down (on large pieces of butchers' paper – which yes, are from the butcher!) all the things children...

1. Worry about
2. Find fun to do
3. Hate about a birthday party or a significant event
4. Like about a birthday party or a significant event
5. Wish they had to call their own
6. Find the most challenging about having a sibling
7. Are scared or hesitant to try
8. Imagine that they are doing

Step Three

Read aloud the list of answers, one at a time. Are there any stories to be created from this? For example, siblings. Children often find that having a sibling can be a nightmare, but then they may realise that they can't imagine not having them either.

Idea Source: Use a Problem

From a marketing perspective, constant discussion revolves around the product development and sales opportunities which are borne from solving a problem. The same rule applies to storytelling. Earlier I made mention of **Raising Confident, Healthy Children** and noted that by identifying areas which require support for your children's development, you may find a raft of wonderful story ideas. There is a seemingly unending list of problems which may need solving. Listen to those around you for more issues. Whilst writers are discouraged from moralising, offering assistance is appreciated!

How do you solve the problems of demonstrating love to disobedient children, deal with death or support a relationship with grandparents? The books, **Where the Wild Things Are, Jenny Angel** and **Dancing with Grandma**, all consider these issues. Now, please don't think 'Well, they have covered the issue,' because a different voice in a different time in different circumstances may deliver support to different people. It is a big world out there!

So what problems do you know are out there just waiting to be solved? What problems have your children experienced or talked to you about recently? What problems did you face as a child? Are they still relevant to children today? List everything that comes to mind, and then go back through the list, to identify the seed of a story idea.

Idea Source: Own Experience

Whether it is a first-hand experience with bullying or an adventure on a family holiday, all stories contain an element of our own experiences. It is difficult to escape the influence of our own experience, and as it colours our world, it is easier to work with it than against it.

Consider creating a list of topics or thoughts. When you are bereft of ideas, refer to it – kind of like the list of characteristics for the Frankenstein exercise. Then simply start writing. It is an exercise which not only helps connect with the right-hand side of your brain, but also relies on instinctively responding to the stimuli, and this can often yield many promising thoughts.

1. What made you laugh today?
2. What did you think of while you ate your lunch?
3. Where have you been today?
4. What is the earliest memory you recall?
5. If you weren't you, who would you be and what would you be doing?
6. What was the happiest moment of your life?
7. What was the saddest moment of your life?
8. What were you most proud of doing as a child?

You are tapping into your own world for references to possible characters or scenarios which may inspire you. An opening about a gross, sticky, smelly banana in a lunch box could be the beginning of a very funny story, as could the dreaminess of remembering tasting a mango for the first time.

When looking for a story idea, you may source an idea from your own diary. Reading about a torrid experience whilst in a totally different frame of mind, and recording your thoughts again can produce a very interesting story. The diary entry could be the story, or be used as a launching point or rather, the departure point for a new story.

Idea Source: Reference Files

Images can provide a source for a story idea. Have a collection of magazine pictures, personal photos or even random photos at hand. Photos from your childhood may invoke a powerful response and give you something very personal to write about.

With the image in front of you, try to make up a story in a 'quick-as-a-flash' response. The more instant the response, the more instinctive it is, and instinct usually produces the best stories!

> The little boy in a Telstra advertisement campaign was the launching point for a short story. I couldn't help but wonder who he was and where he came from. His clothes were rather old fashioned and this led me to think of life for a little boy growing up in the 1950s. Who was his mother, I wondered? This I answered as I wrote, *Two for One*.

It is a simple, enjoyable thing to set up a reference folder. Peruse magazines at your leisure and rip out pages, or neatly snip those images which appeal to you – whichever method is your style. There is no need to intellectualise the process. Don't ask yourself 'Why?' when you choose an image – just let yourself respond to it. The collection can also include lists of words which are accumulated in the same fashion.

When you are trying to find an idea to write about, flick through the images or words slowly. It is an exercise which is akin to looking at clouds. See what you can see!

Idea Source: Music

A gorgeous exercise which can create magic is writing to music. You can go beyond writing with music playing in the background. The objective is to create a list of words which match the music.

When you do the same exercise with a paint brush in your hand and a colour palette ready, there are short marks for sporadic, short notes, long swirls for melodies, red for anger or love, and so on.

Additionally, you can have a list of songs which you already know provokes a powerful response from within. Anything by Donovan Frankenreiter makes me feel upbeat, yet relaxed. The Australian Crawl song

'Reckless', still completely polishes me off and I return to being a twelve year old, not quite sure how to process the world around me. And then Don McLean's 'American Pie' induces such a state of camaraderie, that after listening to it and then immediately beginning to write, I find that friendship is my focus. Find what works for you.

Idea Source: Sound

You may not believe it, but this is a true story from a workshop I did with Year Three students. I was talking to them about sound being able to trigger thoughts which can either become a story or provide a launching point for a story. They closed their eyes, and I asked them to take a deep breath and then listen. Just then, from the building site next door, there was a sharp, resonant clunk as metal hit metal. We brainstormed a couple of ideas, including being a miner, a sculptor, a building site falling down and a puppy being stuck, a new house – my goodness, enough for us all to write something different.

Sound, like smell, provokes a deep internal instinctive response. We are afraid of a horn, love the sound of laughter, are terrified of lightening and cringe at metal crunching in a car accident. Whatever our personal experiences, the sounds which resonate around us when we simply close our eyes and listen can provide an idea.

Idea Source: Previously Written Stories

In the indefatigable Christopher Booker's definitive text, **The Seven Basic Plots,** he explains that the first written story, *'Epic of Gilgamesh'*, is about overcoming the monster. The kingdom of Uruk had fallen under the terrible shadow of a great evil, Humbaba. The hero Gilgamesh, armed and willing, sets out on a long and dangerous journey. He confronts the evil and during a titanic struggle, it seems as though all is lost. By some supernatural feat, Gilgamesh kills Humbaba, and returns to the kingdom, triumphant. If it sounds like a blurb for a James Bond movie, let alone Beowulf, it is; because it has the same storyline. Stories written before can provide a framework for writers today.

> *"The symbolic language in which stories are dressed up meets with an instinctual pattern of response which is already programmed into the child's own unconscious."*
> Christopher Booker, **The Seven Basic Plots**

This is not a recommendation to copy someone else's work, rather the realisation that even in demonstrating you are incredibly creative, the basic plot will pre-date you!

Sometimes, a spark of inspiration for a new story can ignite your imagination when reading an already published children's picture book. It might come while reading new or favourite books to a child or grandchild. Or you could spend a pleasurable afternoon at your local library, reading a wide selection of picture books, and waiting for inspiration to strike. This is not about plagiarism, rather using the inspiration gained from another's work to generate a unique idea for yourself.

Idea Source: The Lightning Bolt

Sometimes, we don't even need to know where an idea comes from or why it is there. Usually more often when you are particularly relaxed and probably happily right-brained anyway, an idea will literally appear in your head!

Always keep a pen and paper on-hand. I have a notebook by my bed. Inexplicably, I may wake in the middle of a particularly interesting dream, which continues playing. I have tried to work out if it is because I am hot, cold, overtired, or if I simply overslept – yet there is no consistent physical state which I can reproduce to come up with the wonderful movies! Launching out of bed and cracking your toes as you collect the doorframe on the way to the computer doesn't help. It is much better to write some key words on a notebook, happily roll over and go back to sleep.

The same inconvenient but wonderful thing can happen at any time. I know a writer who keeps a paint pen in her car, so she can write on the glass of the window beside her! And another who makes a quick phone call to his own answering machine.

And Finally – Breathe Again

Look at that – just as we started with breathing, we finish with breathing.

> "You don't need one idea for a book, you need thousands!"
> Jackie French, CYA Conference, 2009.

Next time you are sitting daydreaming and someone interrupts you – you can inform them that you are 'working'!

Now, back to work!

Time to put pen to paper...

In the Words of a Child

"Doodle drawings are very simple. If you are right-handed you use your left and vice versa, then scribble. For me it was fun because I could make pictures from the lines. When you do this you have to use your imagination. I did. It really helped me with the drawings I did in my book. It helped me a bit as well to show the emotions of the characters in the book. It is almost impossible to make a mistake with doodle drawings."

Domi, age 10, author & illustrator **The Last Day of the Wet Season March**, about using doodle drawings to create ideas.

2 **Write it**

The difference between an author and someone who would like to write a story is simple – the author did!

I am making two grand assumptions at this point:

1. That you already have an idea and you are ready to write.
2. That there are no more distractions to stop you from beginning the process, or if there are, you are ignoring them!

In other words, forget the washing which needs doing, allow the answering machine to do what it was created for and clean off your desk. Then you will be in the right frame of mind to… write it!

If this is the case, let's get going! There is a four-layer approach to writing which takes you from getting down the gist of the idea, to identifying the story within it, to taking note of structure, to polishing it up.

Layer One: Free Writing

When you have an idea, it is imperative to get it down on paper. You can scrawl it in shorthand in the notebook on your bedside table or on the back of a napkin as you sit in a café. Whatever it takes – just write it!

Natalie Goldberg's **Writing Down the Bones** is in the hands of over a million writers around the world. She stresses that it is important when you are starting to write a story to simply record your first thoughts. The way in which she describes the process is very similar to the process of creating a pure contour drawing. That is, don't lift your hand from the paper, don't edit it at all, don't worry about the 'correctness', don't judge what you are writing as good or bad, right or wrong, and just keep going. There is no thought at this stage as to which word, character, plot or setting is or isn't inappropriate.

With whatever medium comes to hand, write words which instinctively come first to mind. Don't over-think the concept, don't try and be a wordsmith during the process. Just write. One trick I use is to type with my eyes closed, reaching into the story to find the sounds, the smells, the taste, the feel of the setting and to push the character as far as possible. It doesn't always make sense. It is not supposed to.

Layer Two: Identify the Story

The words you have on paper may be the launching point for a story. They may offer a departure point. They may even BE the story. The key for the second layer of writing is to identify the story within your words. With your free-written words in front of you, now simply think about them. You are trying to instinctively find what you like about the words, the rhythm, the voice, the energy and the satisfaction of the conclusion. Words that do not achieve any of these things can now go.

Start deleting text, changing words and moving sentences around. Focus a little of your energy on the punctuation and grammar which you may have neglected first time around, but don't worry if it's not perfect. Tidy it up a little to make the read easier.

Then, sort through and distinguish how many stories you have in front of you – you may have more than one! Don't try to cram every idea into a single story, but separate your words until you can see multiple ideas developing.

Picture books are often based on ONE strong idea such as:

- Family friends
- Getting a pet
- Death or loss of a pet or family member
- Moving house
- Sibling rivalry
- Monsters
- Games children play
- Colours and shapes
- Cats and dogs
- Being noisy
- Overcoming fear

Work through it – and then put it away. Yes, close up the notebook and put it into the bottom drawer.

Layer Three: Develop Story Structure

This time, when you look at your writing, you will need to look at it more from the mindset of an editor, giving consideration to story elements such as structure, character and setting. You will also need to be stricter with deciding what is to be included and what is to be tossed out.

Writing a good picture book story is actually a lot like baking a cake! There are a number of 'ingredients' in writing a book which, once combined, create a story that 'works'.

Plot and Structure

From the earliest stages in our childhood education we have had the correct way to write stories drummed into us. The maturity and depth of the writing is expected to increase as we get older, acquire more life skills and having had time to practise.

In its most fundamental state, a story is best described in its simplest terms. I am thinking of a poster which is in the classroom of my youngest daughter. At eight years of age, she is learning the fundamentals of story writing:

1. Beginning: introduce the character and the problem.
2. Middle: deal with the problem.
3. End: the problem is solved and the character is better because of the problem-solving experience.

I know you are rolling your eyes – of course a story has a beginning, middle and end, so does life! So now, let's add in a few more identifiable structural descriptors.

1. Beginning: introduce the character and the setting.
2. The problem: describe the problem, try to emphasise how the problem impacts on the character and why the character feels compelled to solve the problem.
3. Middle: attempt to deal with the problem and make this process happen throughout at least three increasingly frustrating hurdles.
4. Conquer: the problem is dealt with and the character is a better person for the experience.
5. End: 'and they all live happily ever after.' Well, unless you have a sequel in mind, then at this point you will leave your readers wondering!

Prose and Pattern (Okay, so I needed to include rhyme in this section and it didn't start with 'p'!)

The first major decision you need to make with your story is whether you will write it in prose or rhyme. You may already have a sense of which one you think will work best This may already have come out strongly during the first two layers of writing. If you are still making this decision, consider what will suit the target age group that your story would most appeal to.

Babies and very young children adore repetition and the pitter-patter, song-like quality of rhyme. There is no need for a plot, or even prose, but it is heavily reliant on pattern. Children who are a little older do need some 'beginning, middle and end' structure. However, they do still enjoy rhyme.

Certainly use prose for older readers or for weightier plots that have a more complicated climax and resolution. Consider a plot which is driven by the main character, who is being drawn into the impending crisis… realising initial success in their endeavour… the story 'crunch time' where the crisis comes to a climax… the final ordeal… and finally, the end, where the character has undergone some sort of transformation because of their experience.

You will probably read all kinds of advice about avoiding rhyme. This usually centres on the limitations of translating the English language, and the difficulty in getting it 'just right'. Poorly crafted rhyme simply sounds too horrible to read, and thus your book would be relegated to the back of the shop shelf (if indeed it made it that far in the publishing process – and yes, this does happen).

Point of View

With the power of the pen, you get to decide 'who' is telling the story. This is a reference to the view of the story you are taking. It is a grammatical device which indicates to the reader who is the narrator of the story. Generally, the rule is – choose one!

First-person View

In the first-person point of view, the story is told from the perspective of one of the characters in the story. They become the narrator. You indicate this by using 'I' for him or her and 'we' or 'us' where there are references to more than one character. The character can 'think aloud' as well as see the story unfolding from their perspective. When you read it aloud, the affirmation of "I" makes it a personalised story.

"I went to the park one day and what did I see... a monkey! Yes! A monkey hanging from a tree."

The first-person point of view can also be written in the format of a letter, journal or diary.

Second-person View

In the second-person view, the author turns the reader into a character in the story. The reader becomes the narrator of the story, hence 'you' are written to be in the story (I personally find myself distanced from this view hence it does the opposite for making me feel as though I am in the story).

"You went to the park one day and what did you see... a monkey! Yes! A monkey hanging from a tree."

Third-person View

In the third-person point of view, the narrator is outside the story, reporting on the characters in the story, as the events unfold. The words 'he', 'she', or the character's name are usually used. There is a distance and a less personable feeling with this view, which could be very useful if it is, for example, a scary story.

"He went to the park one day and what did he see... a monkey! Yes! A monkey hanging from a tree."

Of course, the choice of whose point of view the story is told from is entirely yours. After all, you hold the pen. But whichever point of view you choose, make sure that you are consistent. Don't chop and change. It only makes the reader feel as though they have gone through the spin cycle of a washing machine!

Tense

Past, present or future? You need to decide if the story has happened, if it is happening or is going to happen. Regardless of the choice you make, you need to keep your tense consistent (I won't start on complicated structural possibilities where it is possible to go backwards and forwards in time). By making this decision at the very beginning, you inadvertently provide yourself with editing guidelines as well.

Character(s)

Of course, your character is not real, but rather the representation of a person. In order to be a believable character, they must have all the traits that a person actually has. Remember the power of the pen. You can make your character look, walk, talk and dress however you want. The character(s) in your story must maintain the consistency of their personality throughout the story, regardless of what circumstances and challenges are thrown at them. A method for facilitating this consistency is to actually take some time out and spend some time developing and getting to know your character. Often, there is much to know and discover about a character which may never be translated into words in your picture book – but it may help with your illustrations!

Write a Character Sketch

Answer the following questions about your character:

- What nationality is your character?
- What gender is your character?
- How old is your character?
- What does your character look like? What colour is their hair? Eyes? Skin?
- What is the most outstanding physical feature of your character?
- What is the most outstanding personality trait of your character?
- What does your character most like and dislike?
- Where does your character live?
- Who are your character's family and friends?

How Well Do You Know Your Character?

After deciding on the facts of your character, now you need to determine how well you really know him or her. Answer the following questions:

- What is the first thing your character does in the morning when he/she wakes up?
- Your character is disappointed or upset about something that happens to him/her. Who does he/she talk to about it?
- Your character goes to his/her favourite place. Where is it?
- During the day your character gets a big fright. What is his/her greatest fear?
- Your character is interrupted and can't do something fun that he/she planned for his/her day. How does he/she react to this?

Settings and Scenes

A setting is physical. A scene is how it feels. The story happens somewhere. A setting can include the time (past, present, future) and the physical location where the story takes place (real or imaginary). It is very important to be as familiar with the setting as you are with the characters, as this provides all the detail for the illustrations.

A scene is a part of the story and whilst we are familiar with the idea for novels, the length of children's picture books does not exclude the concept. After determining the setting in which the story unfolds, the story must now be broken down into vivid and detailed accounts of the action, which are the scenes.

Zacharey Jane, author of **The Lifeboat** and **Tobias Blow**, told me she could 'see' entire scenes in her book, before she even picked up her pen. Finding her voice and describing what she saw was one way to avoid 'telling' what was happening, as she immersed herself in the same space as the characters, as though she was there. This means describing the setting using all of your senses, not just sight. You must be able to hear, feel, touch and taste it.

Good scenes should involve the readers' senses, as the sights, smells and sounds draw them into the story. When well written, the reader should feel as though they've actually been there and experienced the story themselves.

Rebecca Sparrow, author of **The Girl Most Likely** and **The Day Nick McGowan Came to Town**, also subscribes to this way of writing, as she shared with a group of secondary school students at the 'Voices on the Range Festival' in Toowoomba, 2007. Her advice was, "Until you can see it like a movie, don't even begin writing!"

Viewing the scene like a movie is an immensely helpful tool! There are no words, just actions. When you are watching a movie, you don't see the words appear on your TV screen, 'It was a hot day. She was hot.' Instead, you see a person. She is reacting to the heat.

- Think about how you would describe what your character does with her hand, as she sweeps it across her forehead and the drops of perspiration come off her fingers as she flicks her hand to one side.
- Think about how you would describe the listlessness of the wilting plant beside her.
- Think about the shimmering reflection as the heat seems to rise from the absolute flatness of the black asphalt road in front of her and the interminable singularity of the noise a fly makes as it goes around the room, hits the window, then flies around the room again.

A SIDE THOUGHT...
Postmodern Picture Books:

The concept of what comprises a good picture book is challenged slightly by the postmodern picture book. These books challenge the prescriptive 'right' way of sharing a story with children. My favourite example on my bookshelf is **Bamboozled** by David Legge, where the text DOES NOT match the illustration at all. There is no link between the text and the illustration, therefore allowing for a deeper layer (rather, there are two stories). Clever!

Layer Four: Polishing

The fourth layer of writing is the time to add the gemstones to your story and polish it up. The quickest way to do this is to follow the number one rule of writing, which is to show, don't tell!

Show, Do Not Tell

I once had a story appraised by a children's publisher, who said I had told her, not shown her, what was going on in the story. I was the observer, who wrote about what was happening in the story, yet was not immersed in it. I had told the reader about the character and the setting, but I hadn't shown how increasingly frustrated the little girl became as her siblings kept interrupting her.

Wikipedia defines 'Show, don't tell' as an admonition to fiction writers to write in a manner that allows the reader to experience the story through a character's action, words, thoughts, senses, and feelings rather than through the narrator's exposition, summarisation, and description.

This is a concept that is reasonably simple to grasp in theory, yet often difficult to master. A good starting point to learning the difference between showing and telling is an exercise which comes from Noah Lukeman's **The First Five Pages**.

The activity is this: try to introduce a character or his feelings by his actions alone. Don't tell a word about him. Or try to introduce a new location solely by describing it. Don't tell us what it is.

It is a concept which is better explained with an example.

(Tell) He felt dejected, OR
(Show) His shoulders slumped and he turned and left the room without uttering a word.

If you need to practise, write down a list of 'tell' sentences...

- I was happy.
- I am shy.
- He is annoying.
- The sky was blue.
- The dog smelt bad.

And then try and provide the 'show' antidote:

- I could feel my jaw aching as the smile stretched tightly across my face.
- I am certainly not looking forward to going to the ball. Where will I stand? Who will I talk to?
- Even as he uttered the first word, I could feel the increasing pressure on my jaw as my teeth clamped tighter and tighter.
- As I tipped my head backwards, the endless azure void was all I could see.
- As Spot passed them, one by one, the guests seemed to transition from jovial to perplexed, a Mexican wave moving through the room.

Get into the character's shoes and make what is happening first-hand. This is the reason that readers consider some writing to be particularly banal. It should be your goal to transport readers to another place; to allow them to feel or experience something different – all from their own armchair. They need to feel as though they have lived this experience themselves.

By actively inviting the reader to go on this journey, you are enabling them to have their own impression of the experience, allowing for their own collective experiences and thoughts and morals to influence how they feel about the text. If you are telling, you are moralising and attempting to influence the reader's thinking. No-one enjoys this!

In the Words of a Child

"I really enjoyed writing my book. In the beginning it was hard to think of what to write about, so I thought of things around my house and we have a cat so I wanted to write an adventure story about a little kitten. Then I wanted him to meet other animals and have a happy ending when he gets back home to his Mum. I didn't know if I was going to do foxes and bears or farm animals, and I went with farm animals because I wanted Maltie to learn a lesson. I really want to do some more stories about Maltie and make it like a series."

Abbey, age 10, author & illustrator, **Nine Lives**, about writing her first book.

3 **Evaluate it**

After you've allowed your story to sit in the bottom drawer for a while, and you've given yourself sufficient space to become objective, it's time to pull it out again. Let's see if this story is worth pursuing.

After digging it out, hopefully you will be pleasantly surprised and it will feel as though someone else actually wrote those words. If not, remember that stories need to be nurtured and developed. Writing is a process, not a one-time event.

At this stage, there are two questions that need to be answered.

> 1. Is there potential in this story?
> 2. Is it worth investing my time and energy into developing it further?

The writing and illustrating process is nowhere near finished. There is still the task of editing and proofreading to go, as well as the exciting (though sometimes arduous) journey of creating illustrations (or finding someone else to do them). Not to mention getting the book published and marketing it. Need I go on? If you are going to invest this kind of time and energy into your story, it needs to have potential.

You know the saying. If you're flogging a dead horse, it's time to dismount! But if you can see a seed of greatness in your story, it is time to water it and watch it grow. A gem in the making or utter rubbish? We're about to find out.

It's decision time, as we learn how to evaluate it. It is time to demonstrate you know your stuff!

Know Children's Books

It's very hard to evaluate the potential for your story if you are unfamiliar with children's books as a genre. Of course, if you are drawn to writing picture books, it's very likely that you have fallen in love with them during many hours of sharing them with children somewhere, sometime. Not too many people wake up in the morning and simply decide to write and illustrate picture books. But when you enjoy them and fall in love with them, they slowly grab your heart and attention.

Perhaps you have enjoyed children's books in the past, but haven't read many recently. It is no different to any other occupation – you must know your craft. So if the structure of children's stories is unfamiliar to you, pack up your notebook and pen, and head to the library for some well-spent hours discovering what works in children's books and what doesn't.

Read widely and thoroughly, noting all of the story elements we've talked about before – point of view, tense, characters, setting, scenes, structures and plots. Gauge what works and what doesn't work. Consider how the stories end. Look at which titles attract you and ask yourself why they are attractive?

And of course, if you are already familiar with the picture book style, you will probably already have a good sense of whether or not the story before you has a chance of becoming the next bestseller, or the one which captures the hearts of children so much that they end up reading it to their own children.

Armed with a good understanding of picture book style, you should easily be able to identify the flaws and potential in your own story, when you sit down to read it.

Know What's Already Been Written

You will also want to have an idea of what's already been written before. If you discover that the theme of your story has been done to death, now would be a good time to consider how it could be re-written in a way that differentiates it.

Later in this chapter, we'll look at some of the ways you can do this, and still maintain the essence of your story.

Know What Your Story Sounds Like

Hear it

So far, you've concentrated on getting your story on paper. However, children's picture books are one of the last remaining oral arts – they are meant to be read aloud! As you read and listen to your story, you will be able to evaluate it much more easily than when you read it silently to yourself.

Read it

Firstly, read your story aloud to yourself. Sit in front of a mirror to do this. If you know the story well enough, you should be able to glance up every now and then and 'watch' how it sounds, as well as listen to it.

Record it

Even better than reading it aloud is to record it and play it back. While you are concentrating on reading the words on the page, you will not be able to evaluate your story to the same extent as when you can relax and simply listen. You will more easily discover glitches in the flow of the text and identify awkward phrases.

Try to get into the mindset of your reader as you do this. Imagine you are the child having the book read to you. What response does it evoke in you? Does it capture your attention? Do you like the ending?

Ask the Right Questions

When I am evaluating my stories, I have a checklist of questions I like to ask myself. Use these same questions for your own story evaluation. If you can find the words and sentences within the text which answer these, the structural integrity of the story is sound.

Question 1: Are the character's personality and actions convincing?

Even if you are creating a character that has never before seen the light of day (and therefore is incredibly original), it is still important for their actions to be believable. Bravery is bravery, happiness is happiness and frustration is frustration – regardless of who your character is. These emotions translate into the dialogue the character uses, their approach to the problem and how they interact with the setting.

For example, children know that kangaroos don't talk. But if the character is a talking kangaroo in an unusual setting, it can still be believable. The key is keeping the character's attributes and actions consistent.

Another example demonstrates that the tone for the character can be set by using particular words or slang, such as "Um", "Okay", and "Cool man". Straight away, the reader is invited to use their experience of life and literature to picture a young male, maybe with a cap on backwards, who is very excited about trying to jump the tree with his new skateboard!

Question 2: Is the point of view relevant and consistent?

It is important that the point of view that you have chosen is relevant to the story, and remains consistent throughout it. If you are not captured by what you read, but still want to persist with the story, you could change the character who delivers the story. For example, if the story is delivered by a young teenage girl, how would the story unfold if it was told by her mother?

Alternatively change the story between the first-person, second-person and third-person narratives. For example, if the story has been written in the first-person, write it in the third-person from the perspective of a narrator who is viewing the story. Finding the point of view which feels 'right' can make or break the story.

Question 3: Is there a problem worth solving and does the character benefit from the process of solving the problem?

Think about the character and the problem. The more involved the process is and the more obstacles which need to be overcome in solving the problem, the stronger the story. This is simply because the character is more affected! This makes it all worthwhile. There has to be a fundamental change in the character because of their involvement in the scenario, otherwise the reader will be dissatisfied.

Even the youngest of readers (well, they are 'listeners' really, aren't they?) can tell if a story has a convincing problem which needs solving. The story's arc depends on meeting the character in the first instance, then understanding the problem. This is followed by attempts (usually three) to solve the problem, being thwarted each time, until finally, with a final thrust of energy, our character manages to solve the problem and emerge triumphant!

Question 4: Do I like the rhythm?

This is more about me! I grew up reading Dr Seuss books. **Green Eggs and Ham** and **Hop on Pop** are still amongst my favourite stories to read to my children. When you are reading aloud, the words become melodic, nearly hypnotic.

Again – another one of my unsubstantiated theories – this makes the process of reading the book more enjoyable. I have heard fathers describe books with rhythm as a pleasure to read, not only because they capture the attention of the listener, but because they are easier to share when you are tired!

Question 5: Does the imagery excite me?

We are talking about the words used by the writer to conjure up an image in your mind's eye. If you feel as though you can see the story unfolding in front of you and you are feeling an emotional response to the story, then you have done your job!

Question 6: Does the story offer a satisfying ending?

Often you read writing 'tips' which suggest that starting the story at the last possible minute and leaving as early as possible are the keys to capturing a story. I say, don't leave too soon! A children's picture book – whilst steering clear of moralising — is part of the child's formative years and needs to have an outcome which is satisfying.

It is pointless for the bull to break all the china in the shop if he only gets into trouble and is never allowed home again. All that achieves are negative lessons, like 'don't ever get caught breaking anything or hurting anyone because you won't have a home!' No, the bull needs to learn from the catastrophe and his impact on the world, so he can then reconcile this by being considerate to those around him in future. A gesture of kindness demonstrating that he has learnt his lesson would then make the story ending satisfying.

Rewrite it

Perhaps the process so far has shown you that there are glaring errors in your story, or you simply feel that the story is somewhat flat. Work on each element singularly, or work on the overall story. You could experiment with the story and tell it from a different point of view, using a different tense, changing the setting, or putting more detail into the scenes. Either way, it can go through the same scrutiny again.

And then you may choose to rewrite it again... and again... and again!

A SIDE THOUGHT...

Keeping Track of Changes:

As you go through the process of evaluating, rewriting and polishing your writing, changing it a little here and a little there, you should save the document with a new name each time you make an alteration.

For example: EmmaMactaggartDraft1.doc
Then becomes: EmmaMactaggartDraft2.doc

This means you can refer back at any stage and reinstate any previously conceived text, or simply chart your progress. It is also useful to have anyone else do this if they are helping you appraise or edit your work. Again, you are able to refer back to the original versions at any time, if required.

You can also use Track Changes which is a tool in the Review section of Microsoft Word. This means any changes you make are highlighted in a different font colour and underlined. This is also true for changes in formatting.

Decision Time

After going through this process, you will probably arrive at one of three conclusions:

1. This story's potential is shining brightly! I'm definitely moving forward with it.
2. This story still needs some polishing to make it shine, but I believe it's worth the investment to keep going with it.
3. This story is probably best suited to the bin. Time to go back to Step 1 - Imagine it and create something fantastic!

If you have come to one of the first two conclusions, we need to keep working, so it is time for some editing tips.

In the Words of a Child

"I know what Emma means about rewriting. I counted how many times I had worked on my story and I seemed to have so many files everywhere. Twelve different files with twelve different endings. The last one was my real story and it is the one I really like the best."

Nicholas, age 10, author & illustrator *James*, about the outcome of evaluating his work.

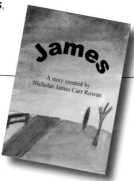

4 **Edit it**

There is a genuine reason why there are as many books written about editing as there are about writing the books in the first place! It is an art form in itself.

It is the responsibility of the author in the first instance to edit during the writing process. Each layer or draft is effectively the result of another round of editing. It is assessing the text with regard to the flow and the quality of the writing.

The task of editing can be broken down into two layers. Firstly, the structural edit, and secondly, the line edit.

Structural Edit

The structural edit is the big picture edit – looking at the overriding style and consistency of the story. Just as in writing, there are also a number of layers to the editing process.

Layer One: Overview

Free Reading

Now you must read it, of course. The first time you read the story with an editor's eye, read it all the way through. Like free writing, think of it as free reading. You are not looking for anything other than the ending.

Obvious Mistakes

Right, now with a red pen, reread the story. Circle or mark any obvious schematic errors, spelling errors, excessive or unnecessary repetition or instinctively respond to grammatical errors.
That's right – just mark the paper where it doesn't look or feel right!

Read It Aloud

Over the years, you have no doubt read many stories out aloud to children, or have absorbed them after they have been read out aloud to you. All of this will have taught you a great deal about what sounds right and what doesn't sound right. You do have to trust your instincts.

Layer Two: Analyse

This time, you will need to read your story with the specific objective of analysing it for correct picture book structure. The overview activities may well have highlighted some potential flaws in the story. Either way, analyse your text for structure and consistency.

Structure

- Is there a clearly defined beginning, middle, climax and end, with a satisfying resolution?
- Is the language appropriate for the age of your expected readership?
- Will the plotting provide sufficient interest and excitement to captivate a readership of this age group?

Consistency

There is nothing worse than inconsistency in a story – starting to write one way, and then chopping and changing throughout it, such as changing from past tense to present tense mid-story. The list below highlights different story elements for which you need to check consistency. Rather than trying to analyse your story for everything at once, which would most likely be totally ineffective, read through your text and concentrate on one element at a time.

- Point of view? Is the narration done from the same perspective throughout the story?
- Tense? Are the words used to convey the tense, consistent throughout the story?
- Characters? Are the characters true to life? Do they respond, talk and act the same way throughout the story?
- Settings and scenes? Are they realistic and consistent.

Line Edit

The line edit looks at more of the nitty-gritty – punctuation, grammar, choosing the right words, and so on.

Layer Three: Review

Punctuation and Grammar

You will be getting to know your story very well, now that you have read it over and over again! But the reading doesn't stop yet. Now you need to read through the story, taking careful note firstly of punctuation, then read again for grammar.

Teaching the rules of punctuation and grammar is not the purpose of this book. However, Bruce Kaplan has done an excellent job of explaining the rules this in his book, **Editing Made Easy** (and believe it or not, he actually does make it easy). I would recommend getting a hold of this book and using it as a reference as you complete the line-editing on your story.

Layer Four: Polish

It's now time to give the final polish to your choice of words. By cutting out or adding words, you can turn a story that may still be sounding a bit flat, into a vibrant work of art!

Cut Out Unnecessary Words

Overwrite – it is just something we all do, especially when free writing. We simply cannot help ourselves!

An interesting exercise is to record yourself when you are speaking. Then transcribe the speech into text. Alternatively (and because the work is done for you) read the transcripts of a radio interview. It is ridiculous how many extra words we use when we are speaking. The same occurs with writing.

Simply go through each sentence and isolate it, taking out words, which are not needed. Find a way to say the same thing more efficiently. When you read the new sentence aloud it should make sense and not sound too convoluted.

Many sentences can be written in a more direct and active manner, which will reduce the number of words used. The key trouble spots to look for are passive, ineffective words like: 'just', 'really', 'very', 'quite', 'perhaps'. And my personal favourites: 'that' and 'so'. If you don't believe me, take it from someone who knew what they were talking about:

> *"Substitute 'damn' every time you're inclined to write 'very';*
> *your editor will delete it and the writing will be just as it should be."*
> Mark Twain

I submitted a piece of writing to an eisteddfod years ago. I didn't even realise I was a prolific over user of the word 'that', until the adjudicator highlighted the word. When I counted twenty occurrences in a six hundred word entry, I could understand why they chose to make mention of it! I actually only needed two in context of the words' meaning! Have you ever looked up the dictionary meaning of the word 'that'?

From the Encarta Dictionary: *It is a grammatical word used to indicate somebody or something that has already been mentioned or identified, or something that is understood by both the speaker and the hearer.* In other words, quite unnecessary.

Use a Dictionary

There is no excuse now. We have access to the most prolific amount of information via the internet and via the computer programs we use. It is a very simple task to 'hover' your cursor over a word for which you would like to know the precise meaning (using Microsoft Word for example). This will yield a result in a dialogue box on the side of your working document. Read the meaning and make sure you are convinced that the word you have chosen is correct in the context of the sentence. This helps ensure you don't misuse words.

Use a Thesaurus

I love using a thesaurus, especially when I discover I have used a few words repetitively and desperately need redirection – and even better and quicker, using the 'synonyms' option found by holding the cursor over a word in a Word document and then right-clicking. This also yields the dictionary, if you need it.

Add Some Detail

I've just finished telling you to cut out unnecessary words. At the risk of confusing you, now I want you to polish your story by adding detail where it is a little bit light on.

Each sentence you write could possibly be rewritten using more detail. Not that you are looking for over-flowery prose, which feels as though you are wading through treacle when you read it. Rather, think of ways you can manipulate the pace of your writing by adding description to moments that are important. Leave the short, sharp (telling) sentences to more fast-paced moments.

- Scotty emptied his bag.
- Scotty emptied his bag and the nuts tumbled out everywhere.
- Scotty tossed down his bag. The nuts he had spent so much of his precious time gathering tumbled out everywhere. A very large one even rolled underneath the cupboard.

Remember Show, Don't Tell

Yes, we need to keep thinking about this. 'Show, don't tell' is simple in its admonishment, yet it can be a particularly challenging concept to grasp. We are so well trained with our oral delivery of stories about ourselves – usually in the past tense – that we say:

"I was really happy." (This is telling)

And yet, we are just as comfortable saying

"I couldn't keep the smile off my face." (This is showing)

Either way, those who are listening to us don't judge our skills as orators. They merely listen and feel engaged because of the personal delivery.

When it comes to writing, it is different. It is imperative that the writer engages with the reader comprehensively and treats them with a great deal of respect. That is, they have the life experience, reading experience, emotional experience and intellect to form their own opinion of how the characters are reacting given a certain set of circumstances.

This approach of showing, not telling, is more inclusive, invites the reader to actively participate and ensures a more developed relationship between the reader and the writer. Telling, not showing, is exclusive, dictatorial and makes assumptions which may be disparaging about the reader's ability. One of the quickest ways to identify when you are telling, rather than showing, is to look for words that end in '-ly'.

34

Telling: "I can't believe you just did that!" I said sadly.

Showing: "I can't believe you just did that!" My eyes tightened until I couldn't see the room around me. I could taste the welling saltiness in the back of my throat, and as I shook my head, the first tear reached the edge of my mouth.

Start to read books with this 'show, don't tell' maxim in mind. You will discover that the literature with which you make a greater connection and which resonates with you deeply, will allow you to visualise the story. The ones that don't are the ones which 'tell' you what is happening and don't allow you to participate at all.

When you are writing to 'show' the story, remember that you will possibly lose some of the words once you start illustrating it. Hence the character example above is drawn with eyes tight and a tear at the edge of his or her mouth, which means the only words needed are:

"I could taste the welling saltiness in the back of my throat."

Lastly, a Hot Tip!

Whilst I am sure someone else has thought of it (I just haven't discovered it in anyone else's suggestions yet), I woke this morning thinking of a REALLY great idea to help with editing. I had sent the first chapter of this book to my brilliant designer and she waved her magic wand and set up the words in a different page size, with a different text format, all in a different font and including little vignettes. I was delighted with the look of the book and loved the opportunity to 'see' the book in its finished format. The delight quickly disappeared when I started reading this 'new' piece of work and discovered many mistakes of many different descriptions.

What I really love about suggesting this to you is that it is so manageable at home on your own desktop. Simply select all the text, allocate it to columns with a new font, turn the paper on its side and *voilà* — you will see your story with fresh eyes!

> Remember to be methodical and professional. As mentioned in the previous chapter, each time you touch, scrub and polish your manuscript, keep methodical records. Date each version and save each version as a separate file name. This will help you keep track of the changes, afford you the opportunity to go back to earlier versions once you have started 'stewing' the current version AND it will give you encouragement when you tangibly see how far you have travelled in the process.

See, the fun is only just beginning. Are you ready now for some proofreading?

A SIDE THOUGHT...

Edit What Has Already Been Edited:

Whenever you read, think of it as an opportunity to analyse other editor's work! Would you make different structural decisions? Have you found any spelling errors or any grammatical ones? Would you cull some of the text? Use it as an opportunity to further develop your editing skills.

In the Words of a Child

"It's hard to hand over your work to an editor. It is the editor's job to criticise your work or make changes to it. You don't always have to agree with the changes unless it's a grammar mistake. It is good to have another person's opinion about your story but you have to be open to it. Editing is very time consuming, especially when you have to decide to take on board the changes or not. I'm always surprised that every time you edit you always find something you missed."

Lainey, age 12, author & illustrator **The Gumnut Blossom Challenge** and **Gloomy Gus**, about the frustrations of editing.

5 **Proofread it**

Proofreading occurs later in the writing process, usually just after the final editing and before the final draft. In the USA, Duke University's writing studio has a course called '*Editing for Clarity and Proofreading for Correctness*'; the name probably explains the difference quite well.

The focus during the proofreading process is correcting errors in spelling, syntax, grammar, punctuation, and formatting. Proofreading, as a process, needs to be methodical and have a substantial amount of uninterrupted time dedicated to it.

The Proofreading Process

The Computer Says "No!"

Once you have typed your story, it is with glee you should look through the text. Not at the words, but at the little green or red squiggly lines (I am desperately hoping it is the same on your computer). These lines indicate:

Red line – spelling error. If you right-click on the word, you will see a dialogue box. There will be a number of alternative words offered, and if not, the option to ignore or add it to the dictionary. It also presents an opportunity to investigate the meaning of the word at the same time, or to alternate with a synonym.

Green line – grammatical error. If you right-click on the line, you will be presented with a different dialogue box. It will advise you what is wrong, and then offer the option of investigating the rule further and possible corrections.

However, you cannot rely entirely on the computer's spelling check. There are words which may be spelt correctly, yet they may be incorrectly used in certain contexts. For example, what if you accidently typed the word 'to' when you meant to type in 'so'? Both are legitimate words, so the computer would not pick up on it. Or 'she' when you meant 'he'?

For this reason, there is no better proofreader than human eyes. Do not, do NOT leave it to the computer!

Print a Hard Copy

Print a hard copy and get away from the computer. But before you do, I have received submissions where the writer has used the most elaborate formatting and font styles, AND I HAVEN'T BEEN ABLE TO READ IT! For example, read the text below. So, now you know – please, no fancy fonts!

> *Even a micro sample like this one can finish you off if you are reading a number of submissions. Actually, even one will do! It is very difficult to detect any errors, like typographical or grammatical ones. It is particularly challenging to consider more subjective concepts like flow and pattern and voice and rhythm.*

To Help With Proofreading

You will need to be able to think without distraction. Don't worry about embellishing the paper at all. A clear font is precisely what you need, preferably without a serif (or a little tail). The line-spacing should be between 1.5 and 2 (just like this section). Your margins need to be generous, at least 4 centimetres. Did you notice this paragraph is not right justified? Justified text indicates it is finished and no more changes are required. Really, the more white paper the better!

Free Reading

Just as when you first began the editing process, the first time you read the story with a proofreader's eye, read it all the way through. Like free writing, think of it as free reading. You are not looking for anything other than the ending. Right, now with a red pen, reread the story. Circle or mark any obvious typographical errors, spelling errors, punctuation errors and so on.

That's right – just mark the paper where it doesn't look or feel right. Some proofreaders go further and will even use different colour pens to delineate different editorial focus. For example, red for spelling mistakes, green for grammar, blue for any queries or inconsistencies and so on. Rather than focusing on doing everything altogether in one go, they choose one issue, find the errors, correct them, and then put the text away again for a while. This down time between proofing (or again, each layer) allows them to reread it with fresh eyes. It is a strategy which I recommend you replicate.

Read it Backwards

By reading the text backwards, you don't allow your brain to make assumptions and 'finish' reading on your behalf. You end up reading very slowly and focus on each individual word. If you want to go even further, turn the page upside down or even look at it in the mirror!

Have a go at reading the following:

> "Aoccdrnig to rscheearch at Cmabrigde Uinervtisy, it deosn't mttaer in waht oredr the ltteers in a wrod are, the olny iprmoetnt tihng is taht the frist and lsat ltteer be at the rghit pclae. The rset can be a toatl mses and you can sitll raed it wouthit a porbelm. Tihs is bcuseae the huamn mnid deos not raed ervey lteter by istlef, but the wrod as a wlohe."

I think you can now understand why careful analysis is required. Reading the text backwards is not as ridiculous as it sounds!

Look Through the Window

Blank piece of paper.   Cut out a hole.

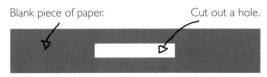

A 'window' is a little box cut out of a piece of paper. Move the paper (or rather the hole) around the text and see words in isolation. This forces your mind to slow down and concentrate one word at a time.

Check Punctuation

Now use this checklist to make sure you have focused on each of the following punctuation symbols:

- Capital letters
- Full stops
- Commas
- Exclamation marks
- Question marks
- Colons and semi-colons
- Brackets
- Hyphens
- Quotation marks
- Apostrophes

A SIDE THOUGHT...
Sometimes Rules Aren't Meant to be Broken:

Learning the hard way is a painful process. I taught the Child Writes program to two of my three daughters in one year and both had errors in their books which we discovered after printing. The first error, belonging to the eldest child was a technical error. Missing text was 'sitting' behind the illustration. The proofreading errors in the younger child's book were the most painful – she had noticed them, but didn't want to tell me because she said, "You had a lot to worry about," referring to the process of getting all the children's books finished! Aaaagggghhhhhhhhh!!!!!

'They met on the first day of kind when there were three...' should have read, 'They met on the first day of Kindy when they were three.' You can see that easily now can't you? I promise you – I didn't see it!

Helpful Tools

The following tools will help you to complete the often arduous task of proofreading, and still keep a smile on your face!

1. Keep a list of your most common errors (or those of the writers whose work you are proofing) and proof for those on separate 'trips'.

2. Allow time. It is a very time-consuming occupation.

3. Choose a particularly conducive time of the day. I am certainly more creative as the morning goes on, yet in the late afternoon, I find I am easily distracted and I start making more and more mistakes – not a good time to proofread.

4. Trade. Yep, trade. Actually, I am not very good at proofreading but I do know a friend who is. When I am working on the books for the children, I will often send her the manuscripts via email and deliver dinner in person!

In the Words of a Child

"Proofreading is NEVER a 'one-man job.' It is so important that you get other people to proofread your writing material as well as yourself. It's like having a holey pipe filled with water. The more people there are filling in holes the less water leaks out."

Nicky, age 12, author & illustrator **Mateship for Sure**,
Glendora and **Best Buds**, about the tricks of proofreading.

6 Appraise it

When you evaluated your story, you used your knowledge of the children's picture book genre to determine whether or not the story had potential, and to decide whether it was worth developing it any further. If your story has made it this far, and you've considered the investment of your blood, sweat and tears worthwhile, you may well have a potential gem in your hands.

But of course, so far it's been your personal evaluation. And let's be truthful, we all have a tendency towards being biased. Every writer thinks their book is going to immediately jump to the top of the bestseller lists… and maybe yours will! But before you pour your time, energy and hard-earned cash into illustrating and publishing your book (or seeking a commercial illustrator and/or publisher), it needs to be appraised by people other than yourself.

In appraising your story, you want to go a little further than simply asking "Is it good?" This is why you must NEVER ask your partner, husband, wife, friend, mother or father. Any family member or good friend worth their salt will tell you the story is BRILLIANT and they won't understand if it is not snapped up by the first publisher who reads it, nor why there is not already a list of prizes in your honour!

What we really need to know boils down to one question: Is this a marketable story?

Take it Public

Who else to ask this question to, but the market itself! It's time to brace yourself as you seek out public feedback for your story.

Find an Audience

It's time to read your story aloud to an audience. Most schools would be only too happy for you to join them for an 'author reading'. You can sit with a group of children, especially the age group you may have had in mind when you wrote the story. Be aware though, if you ask a child a question, they will answer it honestly. So only do this if you are prepared for the reply.

Given there are no illustrations to accompany your text, simply ask your target audience to close their eyes and let their minds make up the pictures. Not only do the children enjoy the responsibility, but you get the opportunity to scan their faces for their responses, seeing the little-knowing smiles of pleasure, without them feeling intimidated. This physical response is all you need from children this age – they simply will not sit still, nor smile, nor beam at you at the end, if they hated the story.

I asked a group of children whether or not they liked a story I had written called **Lily, Fabourama, Glamourama**. Generally, the consensus was reasonably positive. There was one little girl who kept mouthing different words when I read some sentences that were repeated throughout the story. It was easier (and better) to change the words to those she suggested, than to convince her of the merit of my original words. The change remained through to publication.

Find Another Reader

You need three people (including yourself) for this. Print two copies of your story. Hand one to a reader, and keep the second copy. You are the observer. As you watch the reader read, and the listener listen, mark any words they stumble over. Circle any sentences that sound clumsy in the delivery or where the listener frowns or feel like they need to ask a question.

The children do this review in the Child Writes classes. It is really wonderful to see how a child's self-esteem is influenced by seeing someone else respond positively to their words. Remember, any story you write is worth being given this energy.

Innovative Web Sites

In this blissful age of digital communication, a writer no longer has to be isolated. There is a world out there, accessible via the computer. **writers' web** is a site that focuses on connecting Australian writers with readers. Think social networking meets book club! You can register as a writer and then share a portion of your book with reviewers. Then you are in a position to receive some very real feedback. The ultimate aim is, of course, for the reader to be left dangling at the end of the sample chapter, rush to the online book store and purchase the rest of your story. **www.writersweb.com.au**

I enrolled in the '*Year of the Novel*' course, through the Queensland Writers Centre – intending to write at least the first draft of a novel in the same year. The project fell sadly by the wayside and I certainly lost momentum as the year went on. What was invaluable was the feedback I received on my first chapter. The 'voice' I loved to use was heard, but I did have many flaws including inconsistent rhythm and my main character was less than believable. This may sound a little harsh, so I have to tell you, suggestions for research to facilitate a better understanding of how my character would act came thick and fast, as did suggestions on how to work with the tempo of the story. It was a wonderful experience.

Writers' Groups

This is probably not the first time you've seen the recommendation to join a writers group. Possibly one of the best functions the group serves (other than fulfilling social needs in an isolated profession) is to appraise each other's work. It can be an orchestrated process, whereby each person passes their work onto another. The group can determine on what grounds to offer positive comments (never negative). These focus points may include anything from structural feedback to character development, from simple line-editing through to comments about the appropriateness of the pace.

Each state has its own Writers' Centre. These centres can facilitate writers groups or offer courses which may bring you into contact with other writers, so that you can establish your own critique group, or join an existing one.

Professional Appraisal

Sometimes it can be very difficult to step back and appraise your own work without being too emotionally involved. The necessary level of detachment may be easier to hire! Professional manuscript appraisal is another way of outsourcing the assessment. It can be a very expensive yet a very useful journey – so decide what your goal is in having it done.

Ask writing acquaintances for their recommendations. Search online. Advertisements for assessors are found on websites, at festivals, within courses and in the ***Australian Writers Marketplace*** – assessors or appraisers abound. Like everything else we have invested and will invest in the process of book building, work out how much you need someone, how much you can invest in the service and find recommendations for the services which resonate with you.

The role of an appraiser is to assess the standard of your work in its current form, and to apply all of their experience to help you polish it to a marketable standard. They will respond with a written report identifying the strengths and flaws of your story.

You don't want them spending their time (and your money) doing grammatical editing, so you would only consider sending the very best possible version of your manuscript, which has been edited and polished and proofread and polished again.

Use your commonsense. When you choose to engage other professionals in other advisory roles (such as selecting a business accountant or choosing to attend a workshop facilitated by a professional), you most likely rely on a reference from peers or have read something about their credentials. You are satisfied that they are someone with whom you can work and learn from, before you engage them. It is no different with a professional appraiser.

Once you have worked with an appraiser and have received written feedback, you will probably be sent back to your desk to rewrite and submit again. At some point – should the appraiser feel that your work has become marketable and are willing to back their reputation on it – they will supply you with a cover letter making a recommendation to a possible publisher.

> I did that too! I paid a fortune to have someone else read the manuscript and pull it apart – again, constructively. All the suggestions were fabulous and worthwhile and brilliant. I just wished I had stepped away from my text for a while to gain a little distance before sending it off. I would have found half the problems myself if I had put a little energy into it! At the time, I honestly believe I thought they would say, "It is wonderful darling, here is your contract..."

Editor Pitches

Editor pitches are a very constructive way of gaining face-to-face time with an editor in order to present your manuscript AND PRESENT YOURSELF. As with everything you do, always do your research before meeting with an editor. There is no point bringing a letter from a manuscript appraiser if it is not required by the editor, or pitching a children's story if they only publish young adult fiction.

The editors (and often agents) are invited to attend conferences, festivals or workshops. Their industry credentials are promoted, as are the times available and the cost for making a pitch. It is a matter of 'first-in-first-served' for bookings. These pitch opportunities are noted in the newsletters sent out by festivals and writers' centres – another reason to add your contact details to their mailing lists!

> At the CYA conference in 2009, I greedily pitched to three industry professionals. Whist I wasn't focused enough with my offering – rather I spread out all my folios and plans for the future, hoping to convince them I was a real 'find' as far as a committed package – it certainly was a fantastic experience, a great opportunity to meet people and the feedback was invaluable.

Competitions

Competitions often are underrated as a means of gaining professional feedback. Too often, it is the prize money or the publishing deal that lures competitors. There are a host of amazing competitions out there which offer feedback (in written form) for all entries. The cost of the entry is often negligible compared to the value of the feedback, so I would suggest this as a very real opportunity.

> I have a soft spot for the old-fashioned eisteddfod. Most people know about the local eisteddfod in their area. They know there are instrumental, vocal, and speech and drama sections. Many also have a literary section. Having entered short stories into the Kingaroy Eisteddfod, I received pages of adjudicator's notes which were invaluable.

Rewrite Until it is Done

You are about to overdose with feedback now! It is very important not to fall in love with your story so much that you are unwilling to make changes. On the other hand, do keep in mind that stories can be overwritten and turn into a camel if you take a little bit of advice from tonnes of sources.

So how do you sift through the advice and decide how far to go in the rewriting and polishing process?

Firstly, make all of the noted punctuation and grammatical changes. If they're wrong, they're wrong, so this step is a no-brainer.

Secondly, if feedback has brought obvious errors to your attention (such as inconsistent characterisation or tense, or a less than satisfying ending) and you know that the feedback is correct, make the changes.

Thirdly, consider any advice about larger or structural changes, with deliberation. A good rule of thumb is to note whether feedback has been consistent throughout. If your student audience, fellow writers, competition feedback and manuscript assessor are all noting the same flaw, it is obviously a problem.

However, it is ultimately up to you whether to accept suggestions. In the end, it is your story. Even if an assessor is giving a certain piece of advice, if it doesn't feel 'right' to you, you can choose not to follow through. You do run the risk of reducing the marketability of your story; but if you feel 'wrong' about it, you'll never be satisfied by making a change you're not convinced is needed.

A SIDE THOUGHT...
Keeping Track of Changes:

Ainsley wrote a story called **Slow Down, Sarah**, inspired by her own country childhood in which she spent countless afternoons riding her 50cc motorbike over the paddocks on their property. Her assessor recommended rewriting using a pushbike instead of a motorbike, concerned that editors would not feel at ease with the concept of children on motorbikes. Ainsley decided against the change because the pushbike could not have created the same incidences. It would not be true to the childhood experience which inspired the story, and basically she was satisfied with it as it was… even if it meant potentially not being deemed as marketable.

A commercially publishable story is not always the number one goal. Sometimes we just want to write a story that touches our heart and brings us satisfaction. And that is a good enough reason to consider it done.

> *"Remember, language is a beautiful thing… Have fun with it and be playful."*
> Meredith Costain

At the end of the day, remember that the process of rewriting and polishing is supposed to be enjoyable. Ultimately, you just need to go with what you sense to be right, and have fun with the process.

> *"If there are tears in your eyes when you have finished reading your story — it is done."*
> Patrick White

In the Words of a Child

"Choosing a story from my list of ideas took a while. Then I decided to write one about my family. When I read my first draft to Mum, she thought it was "Just fantastic!" even though I hadn't even finished it. I made some changes and then read it to everyone. My sister loved it and so did Dad, who thought he was the star!"

Isabel, age 10, author & illustrator **No Problem!** about sharing her story whilst still polishing it.

NO PROBLEM!

by Isabel Fitton

7 **Plan it**

Now the lovely moment of creativity has been captured. You have a glorious idea which you have developed into a story and the manuscript is squeaky clean. It is time to develop it into a thirty-two page picture book format.

Planning the Book

Layer One: Natural Breaks

As you read through the story, there will be natural breaks. Make a mark when you feel this is the case. It is often at points where the tempo changes or the scene changes. If it was a movie, would you have shifted the camera or changed the setting or the costumes? Use a pencil and make faint notes. The chances of getting this right the first time are not high! If you are unsure about how to divide up the text, remember that the process of 'casting off' is finally determined by how many words fit on each page, given the font you choose.

Layer Two: Page Planning

For a children's picture book, the page numbers look like this:

Page 1	Half Title – A soft introduction to the book.
Page 2	Imprint Page (more on that later).
Page 3	Full Title Page – A more generous introduction.
Pages 4/5	Double Page Spread – There are two pages together and they form a double spread. That is, when you open the book, the even number is on the left-hand page, and the odd number is your right-hand page. The text begins from here.
Pages 6/7	
Pages 8/9	
Pages 10/11	
Pages 12/13	
Pages 14/15	
Pages 16/17	
Pages 18/19	
Pages 20/21	
Pages 22/23	
Pages 24/25	
Pages 26/27	
Pages 28/29	
Pages 30/31	
Page 32	

You may find that your story doesn't have enough text to fill all of the pages. Often this is a timely red flag, indicating that you should actually have more in your story. Find moments where you could be more expressive, and expand them.

If you find that you have more text than pages then you've overdone your manuscript. Find moments of repetition and delete all unnecessary words.

Now, re-do the page numbers.

Layer Three: Illustration Planning

Make some illustration notes underneath the text. Again, let the notes reflect your very first thoughts. The story could be set out like this:

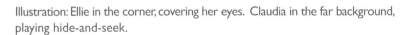

Pages 4/5
Ellie and Claudia were best friends.
They had a glorious time together – playing hide-and-seek and hopscotch or just making daisy chains.

Illustration: Ellie in the corner, covering her eyes. Claudia in the far background, playing hide-and-seek.

After considering the illustrations, you may find that the text needs to be broken up differently. If so, re-do the page numbers again.

Layer Four: Page Turners

Review the manuscript and make sure the text per page is appropriate and the rhythm is not affected when you turn the page. You are looking for balance between making sure the reader has had an opportunity to get excited about what is coming up on the next page and cutting the reader off too early!

Some 'page-turning' devices include:

- Splitting a sentence in two (half on one page, implying a question), the other half on the next page (answering it).
- Using numerical or chronological references, like Narelle Oliver uses in **The Very Blue Thingamajig**, or Eric Carle in **The Very Hungry Caterpillar**.

With this in mind, now re-do the page numbers, if needed.

Layer Five etc.

I think you get the picture!

Planning Ahead

For those of you planning to self publish, there are a couple of extra steps you need to take to ensure you have everything ready prior to your print run.

ISBN

You actually need an ISBN. The International Standard Book Number (ISBN) is a 13-digit number that uniquely identifies books and book-like products published internationally. While an ISBN does not provide copyright on a work, it is the principal worldwide ordering device for the international book trade and library market.

The Australian ISBN agency is operated by Thorpe-Bowker. Publishers who wish to apply for an ISBN should contact ISBN Agency Australia throught the National Library of Australia (NLA) site **www.nla.gov.au** or at the following address:

ISBN Agency
Thorpe-Bowker
Level One, 607 St Kilda Road
(PO Box 6509, St Kilda Road Central VIC 8008)
Melbourne Vic, 3004

Tel: +61 3 8517 8349
Fax: +61 3 8517 8368
Email: isbn@thorpe.com.au
Internet: www.thorpe.com.au

When I wrote and self published my first book *I Can Do Anything*, the entire process of organising an ISBN and so on sounded so overwhelming that I handed over the process to the printers. As time transpired and I learned a little more, I discovered that the ISBN I had in my book was from the printer's pre-purchased block of numbers. When they notified the agency about the allocation, the publication was not attributed to me at all. Given that I rely on my publishing record, you can see why this is not a step I should have handed over!

CiP

Once you have your ISBN, you can then apply for the Cataloguing-in-Publication (CiP) data. This data is represented on the imprint page and provides the record keeping methodology of the NLA. It gives the categories which, when searched by a future reader, will yield the title information of the book and the location in the library. It also allows you as the self publisher to assist with searches as you embellish the original description, hence increasing your chances for being 'found' in a search.

For example, the CiP application for **A Child's View, An Anthology:**

Author: Each individually named contributor
Title: A Child's View, An Anthology, Inspired by NAPCAN's Children See,
Children Do Campaign 2008
ISBN: 978-0-9803008-8-8
Subjects: Children's Stories, Australian
Dewey Number: A823.01089282

Legal Deposit

You are obliged to send copies of your book to the National Library and your state library to satisfy the same requirements as a traditional publishing house. It is a legal requirement and to quote the website:

'Under section 201 of the Copyright Act, 1968 and various state Acts, a copy of any work published in Australia must be deposited with the National Library of Australia and the appropriate State Library.'

I am jumping ahead a little with this last little bit of information. You will read about it on the website and just know for now that it is an obligation you have, so cater for this by printing extra copies of the book, especially if you have a small print run.

It is definitely time to move closer to the book now. How do you feel about sharpening those pencils and finally kicking on with some drawing? More specifically, how do you feel about storyboards?

A SIDE THOUGHT...
The Hunt for Information:

As you know, the internet is an incredibly amazingly fabulously useful tool – WHICH DRIVES ME NUTS! I get so caught up in the amount of information available, I allow myself to disappear in reams of informative text, often forgetting my original task.

Fortunately, the National Library of Australia's website is set up with that probability in mind. You will stay focused as all the information you need is methodically and categorically set out for you in a step-by-step fashion. You can't wander around!

The same can be said for the search for the ISBN information. The staff at Thorpe-Bowker are generous, although I do hear Maria Watt (who has an incredible amount of knowledge) sigh a little when I announce my name...Yes, I have rung a few times!

In the Words of a Child

"Creating a children's book has been one of the best and most challenging experiences of my life so far. When we started we just had to have a small idea, and from that turn it into a bigger one. At the time I loved zebras and so I decided that would be my start. From there everything went up. First a very basic draft was needed, just shapes and the outline of our text boxes. Then we had to do a storyboard – laying out our pages in the order.

Afterwards things became harder. We had to start drawing then painting our images, and finalising our text. Once these were done we lay out the pages, and had a basic black-and-white version of our books made. Then finally when the drafts were double and triple checked they were sent off to the printers and made into our books.

Then it was all over, our hard work finally paid off!"

Lissy, age 11, author & illustrator _Zz is for Zebra_, about planning for picture books.

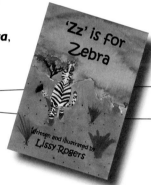

8 **See it**

A picture is worth one thousand words

A storyboard is a tool that uses visual cues to enable you to communicate to a number of people. They are used predominantly in the film industry. Additionally, the computer industry uses storyboards in planning software and courseware development.

A storyboard for a writer or an illustrator is the name for a piece of paper with lots of squares on it! It is a particularly simple to use tool, yet its effectiveness is not to be underestimated.

By using a storyboard, you have the opportunity to assess the visual balance of an entire book, laid out on a single piece of paper. The visual sequence means you can see that the overall design of the book and the text placement have been considered. It also doesn't hurt to focus on other elements of design, like the balance of white paper versus colour, varied viewpoints of the illustrations, and satisfactory flow.

Setting up a Storyboard

An A3 piece of paper is perfect to use for a thirty-two page picture book. You have four options.

Option #1: Buy a Prepared Storyboard Pad from www.childwrites.com.au

We have a fifty page storyboard pad that you can purchase. All the work is done for you. Anne Spudvilas, illustrator, **The Peasant Prince** uses ours! Promise!

Option #2: Double Sided Storyboard

You can simply fold the paper in half, vertically, and then in half again, and repeat, horizontally. You will have sixteen squares on each side – *voilà* – a storyboard for a thirty-two page picture book!

Option #3: Single Page Storyboard

If you hand draw the boxes for a storyboard, it could look just like this: ▷

The drawings to go in each box are only supposed to be 'thumbnail' drawings, that is, small drawings.

> **A SIDE THOUGHT...**
> The Making of a Movie:
>
> The glorious aspect of DVDs these days is the inclusion of the 'behind the scenes' or deleted scenes – offering the consumer more than they intentionally purchased. The exciting thing about this for you as an illustrator is you can look at how the storyboards are used to develop concepts and scenes in the movie.

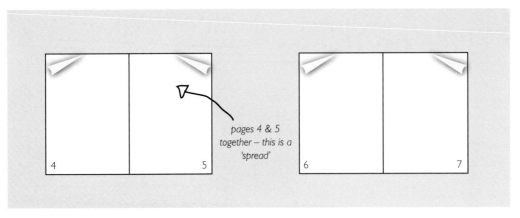

pages 4 & 5 together – this is a 'spread'

In the bottom left-hand corner, number the first box in the pair:

4

And in the box beside it:

5

The next pair is pages 6 then 7.

And so on:

8 then 9

10 then 11

12 then 13

14 then 15

16 then 17

18 then 19

20 then 21

22 then 23

24 then 25

26 then 27

28 then 29

30 then 31

And finally 32*

*In this pair, the left-hand box is 32; the right-hand box is 'endpaper'.

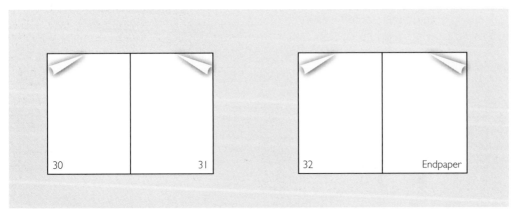

It is really important you leave the half title, full title and especially the cover until last – these need to be your best illustrations and are best completed when you have had a great deal of practice!

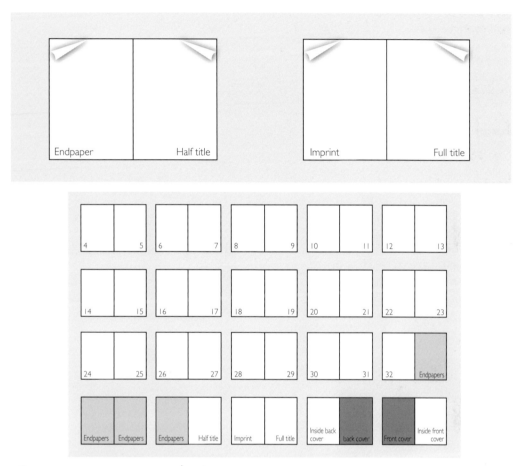

Option #4: Concertina Booklet

As an alternative, another style of storyboard is the concertina booklet. This one is sitting on my light box. You can see the 4 centimetre x 7 centimetre pages fold in and out. The front cover is on the left-hand side. If you flatten out the dummy, it will look like one long strip of paper. Indeed, it is constructed by simply sticky taping strips of paper together and folding it. This is a wonderful tool if you are planning on using symbolism or a motif which flows through the pages. Again, it has the same value as the sheet storyboard.

You now know four different versions of storyboards. One will appeal to you the most. Take it, run with it and customise it to make it your own.

Using the Storyboard

The key to using a storyboard is to not be intimidated by it. Remember it is a piece of paper, so try to get the first version down in only a couple of minutes. Come back and do another and another until you have sorted out all of the problems.

Endpapers

A quick word about endpapers. I realise they are actually used for construction purposes for a hardcover book. By being glued to the outside cover, they anchor the guts of the book into the book. By including them in the design of a soft-covered book, there is an opportunity to create a visual interlude between opening the cover and the beginning of the book. Rather than simply using a piece of coloured paper, as many book printers do, consider the design of the end papers as well.

Half Title

This contains the title of the book. By leafing through these pages, you are allowing for a sense of anticipation to build with the reader.

It also serves a functional purpose. It 'pads' out the page numbers to accommodate the necessary pages of Full Title and Imprint and to ensure the number of pages is divisible by four. Consider the Half Title to be Page 1.

Imprint

The Imprint page contains all of the factual information about the book. It is Page 2. It contains:

- Copyright information
- ISBN number (International Standard Book Number – a unique number for every single book ever published)
- Publisher and printer details
- Dedication

Full Title

This is the page before the story starts and usually contains the title of the book, the names of the author and illustrator (yours!) and maybe the publisher's logo. It is Page 3.

Inside Back Cover

You can choose to either carry through the end paper design or simply leave it blank.

Front Cover and Back Cover

The front and back covers are joined together. They are printed separately to the guts of the book, usually on heavier paper stock and with a more resilient finish. The illustrations for the front and back cover should be the very best illustration you are capable of. Hence it is last on the storyboard.

Now Go!

- Review the text
- Read it aloud
- Look at the blank squares
- Close your eyes
- What do you 'see'?

Start with the box or the structural point in the story which 'jumps out at you' first. With either quick sketches, or simply using a circle, position the character on the page. You may also choose to jot down some words to trigger your memory later. Use a square to indicate where you believe the text should be positioned in relation to the illustration. In the same way you approached the story writing, consider this a task which is completed in layers. The first time you attempt the storyboard, do it in a couple of minutes. The next time, go back over each box and fill in more details. However, make sure that you 'finish' each layer that you start.

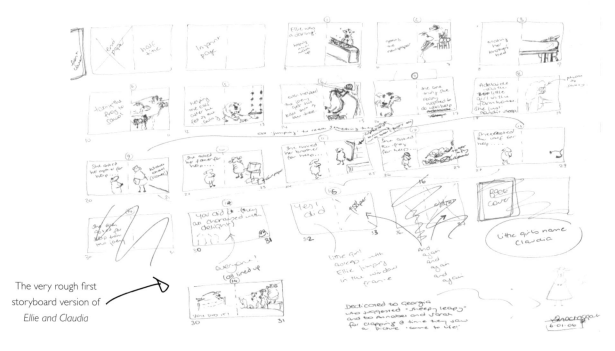

The very rough first storyboard version of *Ellie and Claudia*

Assessing the Storyboard

With the sequence of visual images now in front of you, 'edit' your design. Check the following aspects of your illustrations:

- Repetition: Is there too much repetition between pictures or not enough? Is there scene after scene of the same images, without movement? Does the story connect, or does it jump too far from scene to scene?
- Viewpoints: Are you taking the reader somewhere unfamiliar? Do you have a combination of the following views – close-up view, bird's-eye view, worm's-eye view and distance shots? Or are they all on the same plane?
- Shapes: Do the 'shapes' of the illustrations tie in with the subject of the illustration? For example, lots of vignettes sequenced are useful for an upbeat tempo. A small illustration in the centre of a large page of white is useful for an emotional response like loneliness. A full-colour double spread, bleeding over the edges is perfect for a finale of any sort.

Now it is getting really exciting – you can 'see' your whole book! Time for the next tool, the dummy rough...

In the Words of a Child

"Writing a children's book took many days, weeks, and months to get all of the components right, or as close to as possible. It took time to get the hang of the smaller things. With all the activities involved like blind contour drawings, mixing and finding colours to use with the illustrations, writing tasks and small activities, before even commencing the writing and illustrating of the book itself. When you start writing the book you're in a world of your own. The feeling is great, as though you feel like you have drifted off to the story as the main character, feeling their emotions. When you commence the illustrating you also feel as though you are in a world of your own, mixing colours, splashing it across the paper. And then the sheer feeling of success of writing, illustrating and publishing a children's book of your own, words cannot describe the feeling. So for anyone out there wanting to publish a book of their own, I encourage you, although it has its ups and downs, the feelings are unexplainable."

Ashlee, age 12, author & illustrator **I Want a Friend**, about creating her book.

9 **Feel it**

This *is* such an exciting stage (sorry, an exciting LAYER) to get to – building and then illustrating in your dummy rough! A dummy is a mock version of your final book, where art and words come together for the first time. The dummy is different from the storyboard because it does consider the text and it has more descriptive illustrations.

The main goal of the dummy rough is to afford you the opportunity to see how the text is divided between the pages, where the text is placed on the page, how the anticipation builds for the reader as you turn the pages and finally, the impact and satisfaction of the last page.

Construct it

A dummy rough is very easy to make.

Whilst there are many varied sizes of children's books available in every bookshop, we will focus on a book which is A4 in size, simply because the paper is at hand. Should you choose another size, simply cut the paper to size.

- You will need ten pieces of A3 paper.
- Stack them neatly together and then fold them in half.
- The A4 page facing you is representative of the front cover.
  The following pages mimic the storyboard.
- You don't need to staple the pages or attach them in any way. They need to come apart – but more about that later!

There, you have made your first dummy rough!

Are you concentrating? Ten pieces of paper will give you forty leaves. Take away the front and back cover, the inside front and inside back cover and the four pages of end papers… and you have thirty-two pages! The book – regardless of the length of the story – has to have a number of pages which is divisible by four. Four by four pages together is sixteen pages. This is otherwise known as a section. Two sections equal a children's picture book (thirty-two pages).

The Book Size

Now, this is important. This really is the time to decide on the final size of your finished book. Yes, right now! Whilst in the publishing world, amazing illustrators hand over their work to be set up by talented designers who can manipulate images, you will probably want to keep the set up costs to a minimum and do it yourself. It is much easier to prepare the illustrations as final size and page positioning than it is to change the format later.

So, what you need to do right now is to go back to your local bookstore or library (or forage through your bookcase). Which books appeal to you? The final book size is really entirely up to you. You will arrive at the decision after researching which sizes of books are on the market. Talk to booksellers to see what they prefer to handle. And the hottest tip I can give you is this: take a sample of your preferred book size to the post office to see what the postage costs are compared to books of different sizes and thicknesses!

Complete it

At this stage, the paper is assembled and you can actually 'feel' what the book will be like. However, there is still a great deal of work to do. It is possible now to begin assembling the contents of the page, using symbols, printed text and images (hand drawn or photographs).

Text

As you look at those blank pages, consult the text. Before printing a copy, have a thought about the size and style of the font. There is no point doing a cut 'n' paste of text which is **12-point Times Roman** in bold if you are planning on the text being 18-point Gill Sans!

Go through your manuscript and set it with the chosen font. I am assuming you have already allocated page numbers, so now cut (yes, the old fashioned way, with a pair of scissors) the text into page sets.

Use Blu-Tac or a small piece of two-sided tape and stick the text where you think you would like it positioned. It is highly likely the text will be moved during the picture editing process.

Symbolism

Now it's time to make some marks on the page. After consulting the text, use a 2B or softer pencil and make faint marks, a circle or oblong where the main character will be located on each page. If you haven't glued the text to the page, use a box or a square to note where the text is to be located.

Lines indicating buildings, horizons, backgrounds and so on can be made quickly and decisively. After all, you more than likely already have the 'picture' in your mind and these visual guidelines or notes will be useful for triggering your memory when you return to finish the drawing.

These lines also indicate the pattern of the illustrations. Use an outline to indicate the white of the page versus the location of the image. You will be able to plan how many full-bleed double spreads you have compared to little images or vignettes.

Images

Having chosen how you want the pages to look, now collect images for reference whether they be hand drawn or photographs. If you have an ant in the picture, find an image of an ant or take a photograph. Whether you have a building, a chair, an aeroplane, a dog — all of these objects need references.

I was fortunate enough to see Graeme Base's exhibition 'The Waterhole' at the Science Centre, Southbank, Brisbane. He had the original photographs he had taken whilst on a safari in Africa. They provided the basis for each drawing, and indeed were the impetus and the stimulation for writing the story in the first place. He drew these images onto tracing paper and assembled them onto a page. Adding to this background, foreground, mid-ground information, more animals, border art as well as text. All were assembled. If he didn't like the positioning of, for example, one of the little monkeys, he simply moved it. It was a collage of tracing paper, all piled up to create an image.

When he was entirely satisfied by the balance of the composition, then, and only then, did he copy it onto illustration paper, using a light box. These drawings were 'tested' in various dummies which were accumulated throughout the planning and production of the book. It was amazing to see the process shared so transparently, especially as it was such a methodical and time-consuming process — and we all can do it if we work hard enough!

Check it

As you complete your dummy rough, it is useful to ask yourself a number of questions. If you can examine each page and answer each question with a yes or a no, then you are ready to proceed to the next stage — the final drawings.

- [ ] Are the illustrations the best planned they can be without being final artwork?

- [ ] Are the illustrations black and white? (Use colour only for a single test-page somewhere within the dummy.)

- [ ] Is the text in the right place — on the top, bottom or centre of each page or a combination of different positions?

- [ ] Are the illustrations double spread, single page, vignettes, sequences, spot illustrations or a combination of all or some?

☐ Do the illustrations move the reader's eye from the left to the right (the direction the book is read)?

☐ Have the illustrations been planned for maximum impact with regard to gutters? Note: if the 'finish' of the book is going to be saddle-stitched, there will be no sections and pages sixteen and seventeen will be a double spread where nothing can get lost in the gutter. If the book is going to be bound, there will be two sections – pages eight and nine and pages twenty-four and twenty-five – that will have a double spread, where nothing can get lost in the gutter.

☐ Have you used different viewpoints – close-ups, middle distance and distant views, even unusual perspectives?

☐ Does the text sit on the image or is it to be in boxes?

☐ If the text is to sit on the image, is it legible or does the illustration obscure the text?

☐ Have you planned for the artwork to have a full bleed or have borders?

☐ How does your cover look? Do you want to buy it?

And finally....

☐ Are you ready to start the final drawings?

In the Words of a Child

"The dummy rough is hard work, but it really helps you do your pictures better. You can do lots of planning, make sure the important bits aren't at the edges or in the middle and you find all the stuff you can get more reference material for."

Sarah age 9, author & illustrator **BFF Best Friends Forever**, about working with a dummy rough.

10 **Draw it**

It is just SO EXCITING to be at this stage in the development of a book! A great deal of planning and testing has already taken place, the words are polished (and whilst they are not necessarily final, they are looking good), and the dummy rough is starting to wear on the binding as you go backwards and forwards through those glorious pages.

Now it is time for the big decision: Will you illustrate your story yourself, or will you entrust that task to someone else?

To Draw or Not To Draw?

To draw or not to draw? That is the question. But before you make your decision, you might want to consider the information below.

Option A: Illustrate it Yourself

As with every other component I have shared with you so far, illustrating your book is also a process of layering. By now you will already know how many illustrations you will have to complete and what you need to help you do it.

I really believe everyone can learn how to draw and that everyone is capable of doing their own illustrations. Granted, poor illustrations can let down the story. I have seen poorly written books with magical illustrations and I have seen books written by established authors only made tolerable because of the calibre of the illustrations.

Just as in any other skill we learn in life, learning to draw requires education, whether self discovered through books or taught through workshops and courses. Learning to draw also requires practise. This all requires time - your time.

Everyone has the right to have a crack at the illustration process just as they have the right to tackle the writing process. The rationale we use with the children participating in the Child Writes workshops is this: if the illustrations are consistent, you are in with a chance!

The key to success at this stage is choosing the medium that best suits your skill set and a methodology which will ensure that you finish it. Forgive my focus on watercolour and the use of the illustrator pen – they are two mediums I have found produce the best results in the classroom and are the most forgiving. Whatever medium you choose, be willing to get some technical training. If you already have the fundamental skills, be willing to practise and develop them.

You will need to understand:

- Drawing techniques
- Perspective
- Tone and Depth
- Colour and Colour Mixing (dependent on the medium you choose to use)

You can gain such knowledge through books, local art workshops and courses or the internet. Many successful artists are self-taught, putting time into studying books and applying what they have discovered over hours of practice. If you are not willing to do this, you will find that your illustrations will not be as good as they could be.

Training you in the skills to create amazing illustrations is beyond the scope of this book; however there are a plethora of amazing resources out there!

Either way, I would suggest giving illustrating a go before making a final decision. See what you can really do, given the chance – you might surprise yourself! And if you find that the attempt gives you no joy or satisfaction whatsoever, go to Option B.

A SIDE THOUGHT...
If You Think You Can't Draw:

Many people believe that the ability to draw is an inborn talent… either we have it or we don't. Drawing is, in fact, a learned skill. And ANYONE can learn it.

Again, from Betty Edwards:

'Drawing is a global or a 'whole' skill requiring only a limited set of basic components….Global skills, like reading, become automatic with practice. Learn each of the components and integrate them – then you can draw for life.'

Option B: Find an Illustrator

If you decide not to create your own illustrations, it is now time to start looking for someone suitable to illustrate your book.

One of the advantages of self publishing is the assumed control of who you commission as an illustrator. In commercial publishing, if a publisher were to accept your manuscript, they would assign the illustrator. In most cases, the author has no influence in the illustrator chosen and there is seldom consultation between the author and illustrator. Sometimes authors can be pleasantly surprised at the illustrations. Other times they can be bitterly disappointed, if it's not what they had imagined. Those who self publish retain this power.

You have two options regarding illustrators. You can engage the services of a well-known illustrator, by contacting their agent or contacting them directly. A Google search will often yield the relevant contact information. Whilst you will pay industry rates for their services, you will have the kudos of having their name on your book. If you decide to work with an established illustrator, most will likely request an advance against future royalties, with ongoing industry royalty rates (of 5 per cent RRP). They may be willing to accept industry per page rates, but most of the time royalties will be not negotiable. This means you have to have cashflow, as well as a system in place to keep track of sales and make royalty payments. You must also factor this into your costings and profit margin.

If you plan to contract an illustrator, you will be acting as the publisher, as well as the author. Be sure that your contact with them is professional and fair. A written proposal will reinforce that. They will have experience working with large publishing companies, and they need to be able to trust you as a publisher, or they will not be willing to put their time and effort into the illustrations. Would you, if you weren't sure whether your publisher had the required professionalism and integrity to market the book well, and administer royalty payments efficiently?

Alternatively, you can work with a talented friend, family member or unknown illustrator. You may be able to negotiate an agreed amount, rather than paying ongoing royalties. Some self publishing services have arrangements in place with illustrators who are willing to illustrate children's books for a set fee, usually around $2,000.

There are two points to consider before engaging a 'non-professional'.

1. Are the illustrations of a high enough quality? The standard of illustrations can make or break a children's book, so be sure that you are satisfied that the illustrations are compatible with your publishing aims.

2. Consider the proposal from the illustrator's point of view. Ask yourself how you would feel if you were asked to write a book for a one-off payment instead of on a royalty basis, and decide if this is the way you wish to move forward.

To give you an idea of the costs, the Australian Society of Authors **www.asauthors.org** regularly updates its rates page. As at the time of this publication, they are quoting $95 for a single coloured rough, $900 per double page spread for colour illustrations, and $1,300 per cover. Given there are fourteen double spreads, you can see the costs soaring!

Just like choosing fabric for a sofa at home, or a painting for a wall, you will probably have more luck in identifying the illustrators you DON'T want to work with! You will be able to recognise this quickly, because no doubt you already know in the back of your mind the type of illustrations which will suit the style, theme and message of your story.

Review books in the library and bookstore until you are able to recognise exactly what style you are after. Then begin gathering a list of names. You can also access illustrators through websites such as The Style File **www.thestylefile.com** which is a showcase for Australian book illustrators, and Illustrators Australia, **www.illustratorsaustralia.com** which also displays the portfolios of Australian illustrators. From here you will be able to access contact information. Be confident about your story, create a professional proposal and contact the illustrator you prefer. You may soon be enjoying the gorgeous images of your very own story, brought to life!

Here is a thought for you. In the upcoming drawing exercises, you will be shown how to use a head-high ratio. Using this ratio allows you to spend some time getting to know your character, see how they move on the page and how they look from different perspectives. If you are in a position to choose to outsource the illustration work, ask your illustrator to prepare these same drawings for you. It is useful because you can check, before final commitment that you are both on the same wavelength and agree on the central character.

If you have decided to proceed with the illustration process yourself, let's continue to look at the difference between drawings and illustrations.

There is one important note to consider, in all of this. What are your plans for seeking publication? If you plan to self publish, you retain all of the control and every decision is therefore yours. If you plan to seek publication through a commercial publisher, it's important to understand that as they are the ones investing financially in the book, they will also make all of the decisions – including choice of an illustrator and approval for all illustrations.

For that reason, it is not worth spending all of the time and effort to complete all of the illustrations for your book (or paying someone else to do the illustrations), when a potential publisher may just as easily say that they don't want those illustrations, change the text breakdown in the book or decide they have a different illustrator in mind. In fact, no matter how good your illustrations are, often commercial publishers like to team up new and unknown authors with already known illustrators in order to capitalise on the marketability of the illustrator's established reputation. All this does not mean that you can't possibly be published commercially as an author and illustrator, but it does mean that you should be prepared for the obstacles you may encounter.

If you plan to submit to commercial publishers, my advice would be to seek out the illustration guidelines from each of them. Most likely, you will do up to the dummy rough stage and then pick two or three illustrations to finish in full colour (submitting copies, not originals), so that the publisher can see your capabilities.

You must decide beforehand whether you are willing to accept a commercial publication if the publisher decides to publish your writing but not with your accompanying illustrations or visa versa.

Drawings vs. Illustrations

Drawing is a process of creation. With a blank piece of paper or another two dimensional surface, you make marks in a bid to communicate to the viewer. The inspiration may have come from a scene in front of you, a thought from your mind, an emotion you need to share and explore, or as a tool to help you make sense of a moment or an issue. You can use any medium.

Illustrations are drawings you intend to reproduce. This means the medium and the application need to be suitable for replication.

Many people consider drawing to be what you GET to do and illustration as what you HAVE to do. Personally, I think my illustrations are drawings which I have made in a series and the only consideration I have made in advance is where text will be placed over the drawing and what size the drawing will be. This is why you are in the most enviable position available. You get to produce your drawings from your heart and reproduce them 'to your heart's content'. Wow!

Prepare to Illustrate

Equipment You Will Need

Keep your equipment to a minimum. It is incredibly tempting to keep spending and spending dollars in those wonderful art shops. Keep in mind though, that you really only need a very rudimentary kit to start drawing.

Pencils

If you are really going to take the minimalist approach to the extreme, one 2B pencil will be all you need. Additionally, a pencil sharpener or a Stanley knife is essential. And just to note, the 'B' after the number indicates how soft the graphite is, and therefore how dark it will appear on paper, with 2B being the lightest and 9B being the darkest. A set of pencils are even better and allow you to achieve a range of tonal marks. Look for one with an H pencil (hard), F (medium), HB, B (Black) and 2B through to 9B.

Paper

Choose the best you can afford! There is an amazing array of paper available and with a plethora of terminology, it is best to experiment rather than dictate the product you should use.

Eraser

It needs to be good quality and it needs to be soft. It is perfect if you can clean the excess lead off by simply rubbing along the edge of your jeans (or on the carpet – just make sure no-one is looking!). A poor quality eraser drags the 'tooth' from the paper, which in turn lessens the quality of your finished drawing.

Illustrator Pen

This is one item you will have to go to a specialty art supply shop for. You are looking for a pen that has a fine tip, is light-proof or fade-proof, water-proof, and archival. If you try to short-cut and use a marking pen, you will find the lines go green over time (and certainly can look green on screen when you scan the image). It will smudge as soon as it comes into contact with water, and it will eventually disappear if exposed to sunlight!

Medium

You will also require the art equipment for the medium with which you choose to work. If you are an established or experienced artist, you may already have a preferred medium for which you've developed existing skills. If not (or if you are up for a challenge and want to make a change from the medium you've used in the past), there are many different mediums to choose from, each requiring a different kit.

A SIDE THOUGHT...
What Holds Pigment Together?

The amazing thing about any colour medium is that the pigment is the same, regardless of the medium. Pigment can either be a naturally occurring material or a man-made or synthetic material. The differentiation of mediums comes from the 'binding' agent and other additives which suspend the pigment, therefore making it viscose, and make it adhesive to the support. The different binders determine the application process! Go to **www.dotapea.com** to read more.

Choose a Medium

There are an infinite number of possibilities when it comes to the process of illustrating and the medium you can use to illustrate your book.

Watercolour Paint

Arabic gum is used to hold the pigment in suspension and fix the pigment to the painting surface (the support). Watercolours are transparent and the vividness of the colour is because there are fewer additives.

You have to remember there is no transparent white watercolour. White in a watercolour illustration is the white of the paper! Rather than rely on your own restraint for leaving paper white when you are having a fabulous time painting, use a wax crayon or a white oil pastel or masking fluid. This will 'repel' the water colour paint. If you mix white paint with the watercolour paint, it will cause the transparency to disappear and the paint will look dull.

Watercolours can be made more transparent by adding more water (therefore spreading the pigment). Watercolours seem to be very different when you scan or photocopy the image. I can't actually show you how – because printing this book will influence the colour and the transparency of the colours! As a test run, on a piece of paper paint a couple of squares of different colours, using different amounts of water to change the transparency. When you photocopy the squares, some will disappear! Even though you can see the pigment, it may not be readable by the photocopier.

A SIDE THOUGHT...
A Word about Watercolour and Coloured Pencils

It can be tempting to use watercolour pencil, especially if you have a lot of fine detail. Indeed, you can if you choose to. In the Child Writes sessions each year, there is always one child who is absolutely terrified of the concept of watercolour paint (or any type of paint) and they refuse to use it. We then resort to the pencil. Each time, as we photocopy the illustrations to 'check' the intensity of the application, it fails as a medium. The children simply do not use the medium properly, either by not applying it evenly or in a way that the pigment is not thick enough. The result is wet, washy images. This would be great for a single exhibited picture. This does not work for an image which is to be reproduced.

I have to say, unless you are a master with pencils, like Robert Ingpen, I would dissuade you from using pencils. It is a difficult decision given we are so comfortable with the medium. Pencil strokes distribute the pigment and the pressure of the stroke influences the pigment's density. For this reason, you can nearly always see the white of the paper.

It certainly is not a medium which is forgiving, so if you are determined to use pencils, regularly check the pigment's application by photocopying the illustration. By attempting to reproduce it, you will see immediately if the coverage is dense enough.

Mixed Media

Photoshop images combined with painted backgrounds or vice versa have both been used by children writing and illustrating their own books as part of the Child Writes Program. Both work! One student, influenced by the work of Jeannie Baker, used torn paper collage for all her illustrations. Another student used colour collected from magazine images as his palette to create characters and settings. Yet another student actually used the old-fashioned 'cut n paste' method of printing a photograph – using scissors, cutting it out and gluing it to a hand-painted background.

Another option is to combine two established mediums, such as pencil detail over watercolour backgrounds. The possibilities for combinations of different mediums are endless!

Gouache

Gouache is watercolour made opaque (the opposite to transparent) by adding ingredients like zinc oxide or chalk. The paint will dry to a different value than it appears when it is wet. This makes matching the colours, should you mix your own, very difficult. It is often referred to as 'poster paint'.

Acrylic Paint

The pigment in this fast drying paint is suspended in an acrylic polymer emulsion. Whilst the paint can be diluted with water, it does become water resistant when dry. Acrylics are similar to oil paint in many ways, though faster drying. The downside of acrylic is that it is faster drying! It is not a very forgiving medium for children and unless you are proficient with acrylics, I would recommend choosing it last.

> I have some beautiful books in my library, which are illustrated by Meg Early. She retells classic stories such as **William Tell**, **Sleeping Beauty** and so on, and the original illustrations are huge. They are over a metre wide and maybe a metre deep. She uses various mediums, including gold leaf, and interlinks intricate patterns with stylised characters. She exhibits the originals in an exhibition at the same time as the book launch. The images are incredible!

A Final Word

The main considerations in choosing a medium, is which one:

- Are you most skilled at?
- Are you the most comfortable using?
- Is most suited to the text of the story?
- Lends itself most to what you would like to express through your illustrations and indeed the book?

Once you are satisfied you have made the right decision, it's time to warm up.

Warm-up Exercises

You are already a pro at the warm-up exercises by now, aren't you? Remember way back at the beginning of the book, the idea of pure contour drawing was explored. Well, here we are again! You need the right-hand side of your brain to be dominant when you are drawing. You need to be able to visualise the final image, taking into account where the main object is on the page, where the light is coming from, where the shadows fall, what colours to use, what viewpoint to use and so on. This overall approach is a right brain activity. When you analyse the drawing, the left brain will be needed for its critical approach to the images on the page.

With a pencil in hand, you, as the artist, need to have a perception of the components that make an object. That is, edges, spaces, relationships, light and shadow and finally, Gestalt or the whole.

The Vase Drawing and *The Upside Down Drawing* in Betty Edwards' book, **The New Drawing on the Right Side of the Brain**, are invaluable exercises for demonstrating the different functions of your brain. You need to go and find the book in your library or have a look on her website for more information.

If you would like a little exercise to warm up your 'looking eyes', then simply sit in front of a mirror for a while. Ask yourself, "What can I see?" You will find you will be amazed at the blemish underneath your eye, or how deep the crinkle is on your forehead, or how your lashes point in different directions. You will see the light illuminating one side of your face and if you squint, the shadow under your chin is different colours. It goes on! Spend time developing your skills every day. I believe this 'looking' is just as useful an exercise for encouraging right-brain activity.

> *"Put your pencil to paper every day. Don't wait for a special moment, an inspiration....*
> *you must set things up, position yourself, in order to evoke the flight to the*
> *other-than-ordinary state in which you can see clearly."*
> Betty Edwards

Meeting and Getting to Know Your Characters

When you were writing, writing, writing, chances are you began to 'see' your main character in your mind, and started to understand how they physically moved throughout the storyline. It's time to take this further and really get to know your character.

You must know your character inside out – what they look like on the outside also needs to reflect who they are on the inside. For example, if they have a cheeky personality, this may be expressed through mischievous eyes and a wide grin. If your character has a shy and withdrawn personality, they may have downcast eyes and subdued facial expressions (referencing a cartooning book may help in translating these characteristics onto the page).

Go back to the character sketch you completed in Chapter 2, Write it. Remind yourself who your character is on the inside. Then you must know (and if you don't know, decide):

- What are the gender, nationality and age of your character (or if non-human – what is it)?
- What are the main facets of your character's personality? How would these facets be represented in illustrations?
- What colour are his/her hair, eyes and skin?
- What defining physical characteristics does he/she have? For example, freckles; glasses; being short, tall, fat, skinny etc…

Now that you can see your character in your mind and you know who they are on the inside, draw him / her / it. You may need some reference material to help you on the way. The reference material, of course, will be entirely dependent on who your character is.

> When the narrator is a sheep...
> When I was illustrating my book, I struggled getting the image of Ellie from my head to the page, and it is very difficult to translate human-like qualities on a picture of a young sheep. I set up a photo shoot with one of my daughters! She had to tuck up her dress so it ballooned a little, like a full-weighted fleece. She had to tuck up her pigtails so they fell to the sides, like ears. She had to resume pose after pose as I tried to anticipate exactly what Ellie was going to do throughout the book. It was a very funny process!

Head High Ratio

One of the most important things for you to know about your character is what their head high ratio is – that is, how many times their head fits into their body. Right, I can hear you now declaring, I have gone completely bonkers... bear with me! This tool is so useful for making sure your character is measurably consistent regardless of what pose they assume in the illustrations.

Look at characters around you – photographs like the one I described above, the teddy bear at the end of the bed, the horse in the paddock outside. Use your fingers to 'measure' the size of the head and then calculate how many times it 'fits' into the body. For example, a teddy bear's ratio is usually 2:1, a seven year old child is 7:1 and an international supermodel seems to be at least 10:1!

> From now on, think of a 'head' as a unit of measurement, like 'centimetre' or 'acres'.

Throughout your story, your character will be drawn in many different situations and poses. Before beginning the illustration process, it is useful to practise drawing your character at these different angles.

When you work out the ratio, you can also use the 'head' to measure the limbs, body length, legs, wings, whatever. You have some quantifiable way of 'checking' your character's proportions.

On a single piece of paper, rule across a number of lines, indicative of the ratio you are using. Draw your character facing you, simply standing. Now beside that, have your character assume a different pose. And then another, and another.

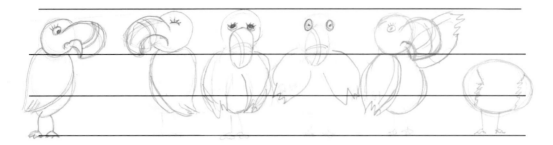

By moving through this picture plan, you can see how your character looks from all angles.

Not only does the head high ratio give you a chance to get to know your character, it also gives you a moment to 'test' the human characteristics if it is an inanimate object! The best example of this I can relate to the children is the amazingly human-like rug in Aladdin.

It really is exciting – you are ready now to actually begin the physical construction of your very own book! Building it takes as much energy and time as writing does, so please, enjoy the journey because although we know where the finish line is, we can't quite see it yet!

In the Words of a Child

"I loved, loved, loved the drawing bit. Time seems to just do its own thing when I am drawing and I can make lines do what my words can't – tell you something important."

Fred, age 11, author & illustrator **Making Friends**, about drawing.

| | **Illustrate it**

You know your characters, having met them even before you saw them on paper. The whole process of a picture book is literally jumping off the page now and it will give you a great deal of energy for what is ahead. The actual process of illustrating a picture book is hard work. It involves taking some deep breaths and dealing with a huge workload, which will seem to take an incredibly disproportionate amount of time compared with the writing process.

Again, if we work in layers and break the process down, it makes it all the more manageable.

Each illustration is handled in the following way:

1. **See the picture** in your head until the picture is as 'clear as day!'
2. **Obtain reference material** which supports the picture in your head.
3. **Build the image** using tissue or tracing paper, and layer on a light box.
4. **Complete the final drawing** by transferring all the information onto the 'good' paper.
5. **Use the illustrator pen** to create the outline.
6. **Remove pencil marks** before rendering.
7. **Render with your choice of medium.**
8. **Appraise the image** to ensure it imparts the message you want to share.
9. **Edit** the image by using a photocopier to check the density.
10. **Accept and store the final illustration** away from the dust and light.

Enlarging these ever so slightly...

The Process of Illustration

1. See the Picture

This is the most important rule you need to remember as an illustrator. Just as you did with the writing, daydreaming time is invaluable. Initially, use whatever tools you have at your disposal to transcribe the image in your head to the paper in front of you. It can be a series of lines or words which give you clues about how you want the page to look. The complication of course, is defining what you actually DO see. The process can be complicated by not always having a live model. The only way to deal with this is to have as much information as possible to help you.

> Draw what you see. When I am doing workshops with children, they are absolutely besotted when I start to describe what the proportions of the body are and how balanced the face is. They also discover what is NOT visible on the human face. For example, have a look in the mirror. The underside of your eye is NOT a line — it is a change in skin tone and is exaggerated by the dark lashes, which are north south. Rather than draw a line east west, simply draw the lashes. A similar conversation about chins and noses produces the same type of response — nearly an epiphany!

2. Obtain Reference Material

Even though we know there is no such thing as a dragon, we do know that a dragon has scales, a spiky tail, can probably fly, breathes smoke, and has a very large head-to-body ratio!

How do we know this? At some point in your reading career, you would have been exposed to a written description or an illustration of a dragon. The image created is stored in our minds and we use this information when we need it. Accessing the stored information is one of the illustrator's most valuable skills.

Information can also be stored in a hard-copy format. That is, pieces of paper with images on them. Images can be accumulated either by:

- Structured planning: I know an illustrator who has filing cabinets with loads of images sorted methodically. If she needs to draw a boat, she accesses the file 'Boat'.
- Needs only basis: this is how I work! If I need information about a rose-covered swing, I 'Google' rose-covered swing and sort through the images. It may be an accumulation of different images – a pretty rose, a rustic swing, combined with a childhood memory, but once combined it becomes a rose-covered swing.

Once your story has been written, you will be able to devise a list of research objectives. This may mean a day in the library looking through books, a magazine moment at home, an internet search or even going through your own photo library. You should be able to gather all of the material you will need.

> Peter Carnavas wrote and illustrated a gorgeous book called **Jessica's Box**. At a CYA Festival workshop a couple of years ago, I was listening to him describe how he set up reference material for one particular illustration. He needed his character to reach into a box and he needed to see her face. He set up a camera in the bottom of a box, on a self timer, and took a photo of himself reaching towards the camera. *Voilà* – the perspective he needed.

3. Build the Image

Speaking of epiphanies! This is what I truly felt I had when I saw Graeme Base's 'The Waterhole' exhibition at the Brisbane Science Centre a couple of years ago (as noted in Chapter 9). The planning illustrations showed the layering he did with the various components, using tracing paper. The flexibility of this medium for complicated final illustrations was undeniably useful.

The basic idea:
- Have a piece of paper slightly larger than the trim size.
- Draw directly onto the page.
- Add components drawn onto tracing paper (especially if the image comes from a photo or other reference material).
- Construct the image.
- Once you are satisfied with the placement of all components, place the paper onto a light box.

Remember – Page Design

- Placement: where is the text going to be placed? No detail from the illustration can be in this space. Note the positioning of images on the page. Is the main character entering the story or leaving? Are they close or a long way away?
- Illustration detail: avoid the gutter and the short and long edge. Have you lost any detail?
- Pagination: are there enough pages for the text?
- Page count: double spreads vs. single spreads – do you have enough paper?
- Illustration types: half page illustrations, three-quarter page illustrations, full-page illustrations, spot art or vignettes?
- Borders: using or not using borders?

Where NOT To Draw

You have to imagine your illustration is actually part of a book. When you hold the book up to read it (balancing each side of the book in your hands), you will notice the spine of the book is further away from you than any other part of the book. Should you hold the book by the spine (supporting the book in the crook of your hand, thumb in front, fingers at the back), you will notice the illustration in the centre can be difficult to see!

The result of this understanding is simple. Don't include any detail or important information in the gutter of the book.

When the book is being constructed some of the image may be lost as the pages are set up for a full bleed (where the colour goes all the way to the edge of the page), or when the book is actually trimmed (fold a stack of pages together and you will see the centre pages are pushed out because of the thickness of the paper at the fold).

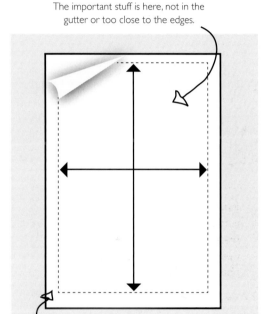

The important stuff is here, not in the gutter or too close to the edges.

Of course, the background, foreground and mid-ground may continue to the edges and the gutter.

What NOT To Draw

I have a problem! Yes, I take issue with one fundamental image that seems to be introduced into children's drawings from around the age of three or four and which persists all the way through primary school.

The sun…

What is that about – the little crescent shape in the corner of the page, with lines radiating from it! I want you to think about it for a second. If the sun was that close, we would all be about to become extinct, it would be so hot!

I take children outside, with a viewfinder – a redundant matt board, which is really a piece of cardboard with the centre cut out of it. With a hand blocking the sun, I ask the children to move the viewfinder around. With every single view considered, the sun doesn't feature when including the ground. It is impossible to do so. The only time the sun is visible in a frame is when it is sunset or sunrise or when the scene is the sky and there is no ground to contend with.

Now you are going to think I contradict myself. But I'm not! Read on!

Where is the Light Source?

Light, or rather the direction of light is indicated by shade. On the drawings, the children are asked to put a symbol for the sun ⚙ in a chosen spot, indicating the direction the light is coming from. You can do the same thing. It won't be used in the final illustrations – in fact, drawing the sun is BANNED (but you already know that)!

We then use our hands, moving close to and away from the ceiling light, looking at the differences in the shadows created. It doesn't take long to realise that a cast shadow is one which indicates an object is sitting upon or above another object. It also doesn't take long to realise that part of the object appears darker if it is further away from the light source and it is lighter the closer it is to the light source.

4. Complete the Final Drawing

Once you are satisfied with the image you have built, lay it onto a light box. You are nearly there – it is so exciting to get to this stage. All the planning has been done, all the research, all the hard stuff. Now, it is a matter of placing a beautiful piece of paper on top of the construction, and flicking the switch on. The light will shine through the construction and you will be able to 'trace off' your own work.

Not everyone has access to a light box. If this is the case, tape your construction onto a window. Choose a time of the day when the sun will actually be directly shining through the window. Use this as you would a light box. Tape the final paper in place, and begin tracing off the image – with pencil first, not the pen.

5. Use the Illustrator Pen

When you see that wonderful crisp outline on images in children's books, it is often created using an illustrator pen (like everything else, this in only just one method). If you choose this 'look', you <u>must</u> use the illustrator pen – No, NO other black pens are allowed!

Simply go over the pencil lines you wish to exaggerate with the pen. It is easy to spot a poor cheat! If, for example, you used a marking pen, the black usually fades to green very quickly and it certainly reproduces as a dark green when you scan or photocopy the illustration. If you use a black texta, the first thing that happens when you apply a wet medium is that it runs! And if you use a whiteboard marker, the paper will end up deteriorating and it will be more fragile and prone to holes, should you overwork it. True!

6. Remove Pencil Marks

If you don't take away the pencil marks with an eraser, the pen and then the paint will 'seal' the graphite and you will not be able to remove the marks. So, gently remove the pencil marks with the eraser, taking care not to damage or tear the paper.

7. Render With Your Choice of Medium

Oh, the joy and excitement of adding the colour!

> *"Colours are the mother tongue of the subconscious."*
> Carl Gustav Jung

Goodness – now we are really starting to get deep and personal. I am not game to even begin to describe what colours do or don't work for children's picture books, because the truth is, they all do, given the particular story and the particular style of the illustrator. The colours you choose will have a huge bearing on the readability of the book.

You will need to consider the choices you make for:

1. Emotive responses: people tend to have automatic emotive responses to various colours. For example, red can depict anger or indicate a sign to stop. What emotive responses do you wish to induce?

2. The influence of colour: the unfolding nature of a story can be greatly influenced by colour. For example, a dark, gloomy transitioning to full colour supports the emergence of the hero. What do you want colour to communicate?

There are two amazing books about colour which, if you are interested, will provide you with an extraordinary amount of information.

1. Josef Alber, **Interaction of Colour**, Yale University Press. Albers is considered one of the most influential artist-educators of the twentieth century.

2. Betty Edwards, **Colour - A course in mastering the art of mixing colors**, Penguin. In this book, comprehensive colour theory is presented by the amazing author of **Drawing on the Right Side of the Brain**.

Rendering Methods

There are many images, on both double and single page spreads to complete before there are enough illustrations for a children's picture book. When you have a large number of images to do AND you are working to a self-imposed deadline, it can all get a little scary.

Working to a deadline has advantages and disadvantages. The advantage is that it forces your hand regarding time management and ensures you are efficient. The disadvantage is there is a lot of work to do in a limited amount of time!

Method #1 Multiple Parts

This is a very methodical way of working. Literally choose one item which is consistent throughout the illustrations (such as a main character's hair, or shirt, or pants) and paint them ALL. Yes, pull out all the pages, line them up, and paint the first, then the second and so on. This helps with consistency of colour and style, as well as making the task less onerous.

Method #2 Multiple Colour

Another methodical way of working through your illustrations is to choose the double spreads which have a similar background colour, for example the sky. Then do the 'sky' on all images.

Method #3 Multiple Images

Working on one image at a time is actually not a good idea. Whilst watercolour dries a lot quicker than acrylic, there is still the potential for the paints to 'bleed'. (When painting wet against another section which is still wet, the added colour will 'bleed' in. Whilst this creates lovely effects, you don't always want this.) So, work on at least two images at a time, alternating each piece of paper, which gives a greater amount of drying time for each image.

8. Appraise the Image

You need to choose a space which enables you to move away from your drawing and appreciate it at varying distances. Temporarily hanging it on the wall allows you to do this. You can use double-sided tape, but please, avoid Blu-Tack. It leaves an oil stain behind if left for a considerable period of time. If you are using masking tape, stick it on and then peel it off your jeans a couple of times so it loses a little of its tack and doesn't pull too much of the papers tooth away when you remove it later. Now attach the image to a wall, where you can move away from the drawing and appreciate it at varying distances. If you are working on paper larger than print size, attach the tape to the top of the image.

Imagine your wall filling as you work on the next, and the next illustration – how satisfying!

A SIDE THOUGHT...
You May be Famous One Day:

Do you want to exhibit your final illustrations (indeed, like Graeme Base), or any layers leading to the final illustrations? Or at the very least, do you want to be able to use your working layers to support author talks and workshops you may conduct in the future? If the answer is yes, then also add to the folder all your working illustrations, your dummy rough, your discarded illustrations etc… You just never know what would be useful to a curator should you write and illustrate a children's picture book which becomes the next **Where the Wild Things Are**, or **The Very Hungry Caterpillar**.

Illustrations
for **Ellie and
Claudia** on the
wall in my studio.

9. Edit the Image

Just as with the text, it is important to check the illustrations, even applying some proofreading techniques. Turn the image around and view it upside down to change your perspective. Look at it in the mirror to see if there is truly balance in the design. These two different views will certainly yield a response from you if they need re-doing.

Additionally, use a photocopier to check the tonal variation in your illustration. Remember that illustrations must be able to be replicated, and if the tonal depth is not sufficient, it will be obvious once photocopied. This is particularly useful should you choose watercolour pencil or need to develop a scene in monochromatic colour. Checking the image as a black-and-white copy is just as useful as checking it as a colour copy. Do both.

Then you can use a scanner and a simple program like Microsoft Publisher to set up a mock page. When you see the text overlaying the image, it may have a positive or negative impact on the illustration. This will provide you with a 'red flag' should you have to rework any illustrations.

10. Accept and Store the Final Illustration

See, you are at this stage already!

Have that folder ready. Whether it be a simple cardboard folder (made to size), or a zippered compendium style folder with single plastic sleeves, it is important to store your illustrations correctly. Keep them away from any direct sunlight. Keep them free from accumulating dust or insect spotting.

Creating the Cover

There is method to my madness! Consideration for the cover needs to occur last. You may have changed your story, moved illustrations, and practised your illustrations over a length of time. It makes sense that your skills as an illustrator are greatly improved, you are focused on the story, and that finally, there is clarity about the end of the project. It is important that the front cover be the best possible illustration you are capable of producing. So this will be the last illustration you will do – and it will be your very best one!

It may take ages to actually work out what you want on the front cover, how to 'describe' the book without giving away the main storyline, and it is definitely worth waiting until the inspiration takes you in the right direction.

For a moment, I want you to close your eyes and think back to the last time you walked into a bookstore, or looked at an online bookstore. The first thing you would notice was surely the sheer number of books available (I had a look at Amazon a moment ago – there were 3,808 titles released in the last thirty days!) The way to make it through the melee is to have a graphic which captures attention. This doesn't mean wild fluoro colours, with a circular book shape. This also doesn't mean you will find that one design appeals to the majority. Rather, the book cover has to suit the genre and the intended readership.

For a children's picture book, the front cover illustration needs to reveal a little insight into what the book is about and who the main character is. This part of the illustration process is similar to other ones in that it is important to do your research. Go to the library and gather up a pile of children's picture books. Alternatively, add to a Google search 'children's book covers' and choose images.

Ask yourself:

- What do you or don't you like about the various front covers?
- Which fonts are used for books of similar topics or genres as your book?
- Which colours grab your attention?
- Is the same colour used for the fonts as well as the illustration?
- How do illustrators treat the back covers of the books?

There are some important decisions that you will need to make before you begin creating your cover:

1. Do you want the image to 'wrap' onto the back cover? If so, prepare the illustration as you would a double spread. Remember the part of the illustration appearing on the front cover will be on the right-hand side of the paper. Definitely don't have any detail from the illustration on the spine (the same place as the gutter).

2. Do you want the images to be completely 'separate'? If so, prepare the illustration as you would two single pages.

If you are not sure, prepare test covers in both wrap around and separate formats, and see which one you like the best.

As noted in the previous chapter, when you are planning and creating your illustrations, you will need to leave room on the front cover for the:

- Title (ensuring clarity and visibility from a distance)
- Author and illustrator names

And you will also need to leave room on the back cover for the:

- Blurb (brief summary of what the book is about, as a marketing tool)
- Review, if available (more information in the next chapter on this)
- Author information – unless included within the book pages. (More information in the next chapter on this, too.)

Important Reminders

Whatever you do, remember:

1. To use the black (illustrator pen) outlines of your drawing as a means for working out 'sections' within the image. Focus on a 'section' at a time – a bit like old-fashioned colouring in.

2. Rub out all pencil marks because once they have been 'sealed' by the medium, they cannot be removed!

3. Use only the tip of the brush to pick up the paint, rather than loading the brush with paint. I can't tell you how many children have ruined pictures as a large dollop of watery paint fell from their brush as they moved it across the page!

4. Use the correct brush. If you are doing small detailed sections, use a small brush. Large sections require a large brush. Surprisingly this is not as obvious in practice as it should be.

5. Always have a piece of watercolour paper beside you, to dab the brush on BEFORE making a mark on the good copy. Then you can check if it is the right colour and consistency – especially if it will be butting up against painting already done. Even if you haven't fixed colour, this applies to the amount of water mixed in with the paint.

6. Always use a wet brush. It is no good dragging the brush across the page if it is dry (unless you are looking for that effect).

7. Always have clean brush water! The reason the water changes colour when you dunk in the brush is the pigment in the paint is mixing with the water. If you have a delicate pink to apply after washing your brush in deep-blue-coloured water, it stands to reason you will have collected blue pigment on your brush.

8. **DO NOT, UNDER ANY CIRCUMSTANCES, WRITE ON THE ILLUSTRATIONS!**
   Well, that is what I tell the children! After all, it is the job of the graphic designer to add the text.

In the Words of a Child

"It was probably the hardest activity I've ever done. To begin with, I thought I'd never be able to finish all the drawings as I wasn't that good an illustrator then. But, eventually through Emma's patience and help, I managed to pull through and I am very proud of how it turned out."

Lachlan, age 10, author & illustrator **The Dognapping**, about illustrating his book.

12 **Share it**

Oh, to be PUBLISHED!

You have written your manuscript, edited, proofread, formatted, polished, planned, practised and illustrated. You may have already decided self publishing is a very real option. Keep in mind, just like all other facets involved in this book-creation process – the more 'rules' you know and understand, the greater the opportunity you have to find the best path for you. Let's have a look at all of the options available. I have chosen to list them in chronological order!

1. Conventional Trade Publishing
2. Print on Demand Publishing
3. Subsidy Publishing
4. Vanity Publishing
5. Self Publishing
6. eBooks

Before going into each in detail, I have to share words of wisdom from Stephanie Dale, **My Pilgrims Heart** and **Hymn for the Wounded Man**. "It is about navigating the right path for your project. Rather than limiting your actions by your own fears, acknowledge there are no mistakes to be made in this process – you are simply on a remarkable journey."

1. Conventional Trade Publishing

This is where you write your manuscript and then look to the outside world for someone to help turn it into a book. Conventional trade publishers take the financial risk and do all the work for you – editing, printing, wholesaling, distributing and marketing, using established distribution channels to get the book into the hands of the readers. The sales and administrative side of things is their responsibility (saving you a lot of time). All you have to do is plan to spend the advance and then float on the royalties that come in! Mmmm… I can see the appeal.

On the other hand, the publishing company also takes the largest share of the profits for their efforts. And you are also beholden to the time constraints and deadlines of a larger organisation over which you have limited control and input. But if you do not have the time or the confidence to pursue self publishing, this could be the option for you.

To Pursue Conventional Trade Publishing

If you want to pursue the conventional trade publishing route, you will need to be willing to hand over control of your precious manuscript and illustrations to the publisher. As the publisher is taking the financial risk and is an industry professional, they will make the decisions regarding all aspects of the book creation and publication process, including choice of illustrator and length of time in print. While you may be consulted, there are no guarantees that you will be.

Regarding illustrations, if you're going to go down this road of creating your own, it is best not to complete all the illustrations first, as the publisher may not decide to use them, or may edit and change the layout of the text and therefore the page breaks and illustrations for each page. Submit dummy rough with one finished illustration demonstrating the rendering technique you want to use.

The income you can hope to achieve is a down payment then a standard industry royalty amount is 10 per cent of the recommended retail price (in other words $1.95 of a book which sells for $19.95). You will only receive half of that again if you are not the author / illustrator. On the other hand, conventional publishing does save you the headache of having to tend to the administrative details that come with self publishing – and you can then be free to get on with writing your next book.

Realise that this option will require your patience. It can take some time to secure a publishing contract, as it is not unusual to wait a few months to hear back from a publisher to whom you've sent your manuscript for consideration.

If you have weighed up the pros and cons and you're ready to go with conventional publishing, read on to see the steps you will need to take.

Step One: Find the Right Publisher for You

This can become a very pleasant task. Go down to your local bookstore. As you browse through the books, happily inhaling the words produced (as you know, after many hours of hard work), keep looking for books 'just like yours'. A quick glance at the imprint page (the one with the small type usually at the beginning of the book) will supply the publisher's name and contact information. If they have published that type of book before, you are increasing your chances of presenting a book they may be interested in. There is absolutely no point in sending a children's picture book to an academic publisher, or even a rhyming picture book to a publisher who tends to only publish prose.

Alternatively, you can do a Google search or purchase resources like the must-have **The Australian Writer's Marketplace**, produced biennially by the Queensland Writers Centre. This reference material can also be accessed via an annual online subscription. It lists publishers, agents, manuscript appraisers, magazines and journals, competitions, you name it. If it is relevant to a writer – it is there!

Step Two: Read the Publishers' Website

With the information in hand, you have an internet research list for when you return to your computer. Now it's time to read the publisher's websites to glean all of the information you will need to create a targeted and impressive submission.

You will find submission guidelines clearly noted in one of the tabs on the home page. Publishers are used to getting literally thousands and thousands of manuscripts – and subsequently, the information shared is usually prescriptive.

It is important to invest a little energy into finding the name of the children's picture book editor you are sending your manuscript to. This sure beats 'Dear Sir/Madam' when you are writing the salutation on your cover letter.

In addition, look for the publisher's professional main aim, and then prepare your submission to highlight the 'matches' between their purpose and your story. This may be clearly noted on their website, or you may have to dig a little bit for it. For example, New Frontier's website clearly states: 'New Frontier publishes quality children's and educational books which inspire, educate and uplift children'. If you were submitting to New Frontier, you would ask yourself how your story inspires, educates and uplifts children, and communicate this in your cover letter. It is a waste of your and the publisher's time and energy if your book and the publishing house don't even remotely match.

You may find that when you research a publisher's website, they may not currently be accepting unsolicited submissions. An unsolicited submission is one that has been initiated by the author, rather than at the request of the publisher. Don't be discouraged by this. Sure, it means that you should not send your manuscript to them. But there is no reason why you cannot send a one-page query letter, giving a brief blurb on your book, and allowing the publisher to request you send it to them.

Step Three: Do Exactly What They Tell You

The manuscript needs to be accompanied by a cover letter briefly introducing youself, your experience and your commitment to the industry. It is also an opportunity to share why you have chosen to send your work to them. You may be asked to include a synopsis of the book – like a blurb, only with a bit more insight. Again, keep it brief, catchy and interesting. Editors can read many submissions each day – make yours stand out! Include a self-addressed stamped envelope. This makes it so much easier for the publisher to return your manuscript or to tell you they LOVE YOUR WORK! If you have a longer list of professional credentials (and this could include courses, competition successes, published articles etc.), you may want to consider a separate bio page. Make it an interesting read, but do not exaggerate the truth.

Consider the presentation – Make sure the manuscript is presented in pristine condition:

- Use white, clean paper.
- Ensure the printing is clear, with no smudges or marks.
- Make your text double spaced (hence easier for the editor to make notes on the manuscript. It is OK to use single spacing for your cover letter).
- Use left-aligned text, not justified as this indicates that you are open to editing.
- Ensure your manuscript is free of typographical and grammatical errors.
- Do not bind it. If anything, use a large paperclip.
- Do not embellish it.
- Send copies of artwork – not original illustrations. The editor will request the originals if they want to see them.

You must also decide whether you are going to give first consideration to a specific publisher, or if you will send multiple submissions at the one time. There is a massive debate out there regarding multiple submissions. You can talk to any agent or publisher and each will have their own opinion about whether it is appropriate or not. It is a good question for you to ask when you contact the publisher to check if they are still accepting unsolicited submissions.

If you choose to send your manuscript to a number of publishers at a time, make mention of this in your cover letter. Some publishers acknowledge the timeframes involved in assessing the suitability of a manuscript and the reply time; and therefore they understand, and may even recommend, sending multiple submissions. However, some publishers want to be the only publisher considering a manuscript.

Take notice of what the publisher's website says in relation to letters of recommendation from manuscript appraisal agencies. If you have a letter of recommendation from a manuscript appraisal agency, include it in your submission unless the publisher's website says specifically not to include it.

Each publisher has different (and seemingly conflicting rules), but they are a means to an end. There are an incalculable number of manuscripts sitting in slush piles on desks around the globe. There is only so much time in the day. Given those in the industry are passionate about books and about reading, it stands to reason they are definitely interested in finding manuscripts which have merit – and they eventually will, if it is in the pile.

> I was at the Byron Bay Writers' Festival in 2007, listening to Alexandra Ardonetto speak about her experiences. She was fourteen! Having written a book for young adults, she researched publishers, chose Harper Collins, followed the guidelines to the letter and received a reply twenty weeks later. I listened to her publisher, Lisa Berryman, who said Alexandra's manuscript was retrieved from the slush pile and she had indeed followed the guidelines to a tee!

So, does that all sound manageable?

It is a bit like dealing with the 'rules' in any facet of creative life. Know the rules, and then work out which ones you can break! It certainly helps if you are honest and being yourself, rather than using a prescriptive suggestion which worked for someone else.

> A dear friend gave me a book that was written and illustrated by a very good friend of hers. I loved it, my children loved it, and we were thrilled as the next couple of books in the series were released. It was wonderful to then later read an essay in The Australian Writers Marketplace written by the same author – the now very successful Annie O'Dowd. She talks about sending out fifty submissions before being accepted. She stuck with the publishers requested format each time. But in a bid to grab the attention of the possible 'weary assistant', she actually sent her fully illustrated desktop-published manuscript in a beautiful wooden box. She even included a soft toy! My pin-up girl when it comes to knowing the rules and then breaking them.

Step Four: Keep Writing

So what do you do while you are waiting for a response from a publisher? Keep writing! It takes ages for the wheels of the publishing industry to turn and there is absolutely no point in sitting around waiting for the reply, good or bad. Whether you have elected to make a single submission or multiple submissions, you need to allow time for your manuscript to make it to the top of the 'slush pile'. What if you concentrate all of your energy on waiting to hear from the editor, only to receive a rejection letter (which is quite possible)? It will be even harder to get back into writing once you're feeling discouraged. Instead, go out and write your next bestseller. It's far easier to deal with a rejection when you have your next story in hand.

Step Five: Follow Up

The publisher's submission guidelines will give you an indication of the timeframe they work with. Whether it is three or six months, don't hesitate to contact them if you haven't heard from them after that timeframe. Chances are, you won't be speaking to the powers that be, rather you will have to have your fingers and toes crossed just to get through the secretary or the receptionist! Remember not to be a pest though – these people are just as busy as you are!

Step Six: Don't be Seduced by Short Cuts

It is very interesting to spend some 'internet' time researching all the options available for writers, in a bid to having your manuscript published. Every writer believes their story is the one that should be heard, yet the conventional publishing industry is notoriously difficult to break into. As you submit your manuscript, wait for weeks and weeks (or months and months), only to have it returned, the cyclical process can become fatiguing after a while. It is no wonder thousands and thousands of writers are falling for the publishing scams flourishing on the internet. It only takes a relatively simple search request like 'publishing children's picture books' and *voilà* – you will have pages of 'publishers' who will be appealing directly to you. If they are, steer clear!

Step Seven: Don't Give Up!

There are different publishers, and their role is to be a gatekeeper of style and form, ensuring that quality writing makes it to the bookshelf, and that which is below standard does not! You have already decided this is the option for you. However, there are many possible reasons for rejection that are not necessarily your writing:

- The book is generally not the type published by the publisher (avoid by doing research).
- The book doesn't fit into the publisher's pre-determined list.
- A similar book or a similar theme was published recently (check new and upcoming releases).
- The editor may simply just not like it.

When – not if – you receive a standard rejection letter, realise that you are not alone. There isn't an author or illustrator alive who hasn't experienced one of these. If you receive a rejection letter which actually explains why your manuscript was not accepted (and these are rare), consider that an encouragement, not a disappointment. The suggestions made by the editor can direct you through the rewrite and hopefully they will be open to a resubmission.

More often than not, you will receive a 'with compliments' slip attached to your manuscript or a proforma letter with your name inserted into it, and no explanations. Keep them in a file. You never know when this information will be handy.

2. Print on Demand Publishing (POD)

This publishing model is AND WAS a product of changes in technology. Consider this: whilst paper was invented in China in around 1 AD and books were indeed printed, in the very early days of books in Europe only the wealthy could afford books. This is because they were produced entirely by hand, a single copy at a time. There were no considerations for copyright or publishing rights. You could pay to have a text copied. It wasn't until the Gutenberg press was invented in around 1440 that books became the industrial construct they are today, effectively superseding produce on demand.

So, we have effectively travelled a full circle. Now, it is possible to print a small quantity of books – even a single copy at a time – because of another technological invention, digital printing. The book can be promoted on the internet, and as orders are received, the book can be printed and distributed directly to the purchasers. The elimination of warehousing, stock, wholesalers and distributors has broken significant barriers which prevented many entering the traditional publishing industry. With POD, there isn't the huge outlay for a large volume of stock. Keep in mind though, this does mean the economies of scale achieved with offset printing are also forfeited.

To Pursue Print on Demand Publishing

Having parked in my garage with 1,000 books in boxes lining the walls and being unable to open the car door, the idea of only having books printed to order just as they are sold is a VERY appealing option.

There are particularly strict guidelines regarding the set up of the books – a necessity given that the POD suppliers do not accept anything other than a print ready PDF file. If they do offer any other services, proofreading, book set-up and so on, it would be for an establishment fee. Not all POD printers check the product as it is printed.

A SIDE THOUGHT...

According to Andre Bernard in his book, **Rotten Rejections**, editors don't always get it right:

- Dr Seuss received the advice that his manuscript was 'too different from other juveniles on the market to warrant its selling'.
- **The Tale of Peter Rabbit** was turned down so many times, Beatrix Potter initially self published it.
- **The Wind in the Willows** by Kenneth Grahame was described as 'an irresponsible holiday story'.

Each of these stories has gone on to be hugely successful. So if you receive a rejection letter, take out anything useful you can from it… and then move on.

When I asked someone 'in the know' – they may have mentioned most POD suppliers can be found under their previous name in the Yellow Pages – 'PRINTERS'.

Derrrrr, of course! The change in perception comes from the changes in technology from offset printing to quality digital printing.

The main benefit of POD is the low entry cost. It is more relevant to a fiction novel rather than a full-colour children's picture book. Time will tell! If you really want to travel this road, you can explore the offering of Booksurge or Lightning, Lulu or Blurb, which are some of the businesses out there offering POD services. To make sure you get the best out of this technology, only work with those who don't charge any service fees, just the printing costs. Remember, you need to be print-ready. If you don't set-up your book and have arrived at the printers with loose illustrations and text to be retyped and design elements still not addressed, of course you would be charged a set-up fee.

> One POD I have used is **www.blurb.com**. I have produced a cook book with a limited print run of only twenty copies, and a memoir for a friend, ***Eggs Contradict***. The later is available in the Blurb bookshop for family and friends. The quality of the product is remarkable and the organisation is great to deal with. The binding was flawed in the first batch of hard cover cookbooks. I took photos of the damaged product, and within an hour of sending it, received notification via email from the printers that a reprint of the entire batch was ordered and postage covered. You can't get better than that!
>
> I did start with setting up an account with another US POD. The governance and the expectations from the printers were weighty to say the least and the pricing information was only in UK pounds or US dollars. Translating the cost into AUD was too onerous and distracting a task given it was itemised, not just for a thirty-two page picture book! Additionally, there was a prohibitive postage cost for transporting books from the UK or the US. I haven't investigated Asia or India, but POD is a relatively under-utilised print option in Australia.

When a POD business offers you a 'package' where 'professional designers will ensure your product sells in a crowded market place', or 'sales are generated because of inclusion on Amazon's lists' then take another look at the offering – it is actually subsidy publishing!

3. Subsidy Publishing

There are two sides to subsidy publishing. The first is really a mature version of vanity publishing. You pay a proportion of the set-up and marketing costs for the production of your book, and these are redeemable once you reach a predetermined sales volume. The second is a genuine offering from businesses involved in the publishing industry who are subsequently offering their in-house services to self publishers. This allows them to generate another income stream, separate from their own book sales business. The services are all fundamental in the book creation process. Broken down, the offering may include manuscript appraisal, editing and proofreading, actually setting up the books and printing, through to marketing and sales support. You shouldn't be sending a book out there, into the wilderness, without considering these elements.

To Pursue Subsidy Publishing

If you are tempted to follow this path, please be very cautious and investigate the company before handing over a cent.

How do you avoid a scam? The first indicator is conventional wisdom: 'If it sounds too good to be true, it probably is!' You are a writer after all – you have a finely developed sense of awareness. Apply it now.

- Use your common sense; if the 'publisher' doesn't even use your name in reply emails, they are only interested in your money, not in developing a relationship with you.
- If the reply is unusually immediate – especially as you sit at your desk with sunlight streaming in on your face, and a reply comes from a publisher on the other side of the world IN THE MIDDLE OF THE NIGHT – and it is a form letter – well, they are not really genuine, are they?
- If the reply is unusually immediate (and the warning bell is already ringing because of the above point) AND you are offered a 'joint venture', well, truly – add the email address to your 'do-not-let-it-in' junk folder address list. Now you know exactly what they are looking for – yes, your money.
- Just as you discovered the publisher on the net, so too can you unearth a scam. It just takes a little more time. The wonderful thing about a writer scorned, is they will write about it. A simple Google search will yield hundreds of blog sites or blurts (as I like to call the more aggressive postings) telling you exactly what their experience is. Read them and take them on-board.

An indispensable website for you to go to and read, read, read as much content as your mind can bear is that of the Science Fiction Writers Association in the USA. They have a vast amount of information about corrupt business practices, including outcomes of a trial where the judgement was against the business, for the author. **www.sfwa.org/for-authors/writer-beware**

Another checking mechanism described by author Stephanie Dale is to simply Google the name of the business / organisation / individual followed by the word SCAM – if there is a problem, you will find it!

4. Vanity Publishing

Vanity publishers exist to profiteer from the client – you, the wistful writer. You will be told, "Of course we will publish your book," and you will have to pay a little for the editing and the printing and the distribution and the promotion, but truly, you will be GUARANTEED links to Amazon, all the biggest and best bookstores, thousands of reviews, billions of readers online. What could possibly go wrong?

To Pursue Vanity Publishing

I say "DON'T!" (Yes, I am shouting!) These publishers operate primarily to make a profit from the author, not from book sales. The services offered are valid and important in the process of constructing a book – editorial support, printing liaison, distribution options, marketing considerations and more. The problem is promises of incredible book sales because your book is on an Amazon list or because of their distribution contacts, can often fall short of expectations.

```
> Hello!>
> Last month I sent you an email to let you know that your manuscript
> was entering final review. I asked that you respond to my e-mail and
> answer a few questions which would help in our review.
```

You can understand why, in this litigious world we live in, I am not going to tell you exactly who wrote this! The vanity publisher offered me the 'opportunity' to have my manuscript published, which was amazing given there are tens of thousands of writers to whom they don't offer this opportunity. All I have to do is make an 'author investment' of $3,985 which covers everything – production, editing, layout, cover design, online marketing, nationwide distribution, promotion, book signings, free book offers, a lifetime 60 per cent off purchasing status, free audio and eBook production and much more. When I sell 5,000 copies, I will receive the deposit back. What could possibly go wrong?!?!

5. Self Publishing

When self publishing, you do it all yourself. Write the words, draw the pictures (or find an illustrator), decide on the graphic layout of the book and the cover, negotiate with the printers, pick up the books and start shipping them to customers or bookstores, organise the marketing – and reap ALL the rewards! You can choose the traditional book format (printed pages within a paperback or hard cover), use print on demand (POD) publishing, or the eBook.

To Pursue Self Publishing

I know I said earlier that one of the valuable roles of conventional publishers is to be gatekeepers and to make sure our shelves – both literal and virtual – are not breaking with the strain of too many poorly chosen words. Thank goodness!

However (and this is a biggie), if you genuinely believe in your book, can see it on shelves around the country and can't imagine not finishing the project yourself OR you are driven to give a gift of words to others, then self publishing is a very real and attainable option.

The Benefits of Self Publishing:

Shorter Timeframe

I have just read the submission guidelines for a well-known publisher. They are only accepting unsolicited manuscripts after October (it is July now) – twelve weeks before it can be sent. Their current reply-time has blown out from twelve weeks to sixteen, because of the massive volume received. That equals twenty-eight weeks plus to find out if you are rejected! Instead of taking so long for your manuscript to be assessed and appraised for its marketability, you can be handing a personalised gift to your children, grandchildren, nieces or nephews within a matter of months. For some people, this is incredibly important.

"A person could literally die waiting for a publisher to pick up their story.
Endless knockbacks and long delays weren't on my agenda as I was undergoing
chemotherapy for breast cancer at the time of publishing my book.
By doing it myself I could have control over the whole process."

Effervescent and invincible self publisher, Deb Pacholke, **Eric the Echidna**, 2009

Maintaining Control

As a self publisher, you can choose the cover design, the final illustrations, where the text is positioned, how long the dedication is, book launch dates, who receives the galley, how many copies you can give away or donate for prizes, whether or not you reprint… the list goes on!

Higher Income

The money which potentially can be generated from self publishing is remarkable! Let's assume you have just received your quote from the printer. You are printing 1,000 copies of a thirty-two page picture book for $3.70 a copy. You can sell it for $14.95. Straight away, your margin is $11.25 or 75 per cent. I believe $10,000 plus would be adequate reward for stomping around bookstores, begging them to take copies on consignment, setting up author visits at schools and doing book-signings, hawking your wares at the markets, setting up a website for sales – and that's just the first print run! You're always able to print another run (even a larger one if your book has proven successful), for further profit.

The Feedback

I believe this is one of the most rewarding aspects of self publishing. You are actually talking to those who purchase your book and actually read the book. I still have people who bought my first book in 2003 who tell me how their children or grandchildren enjoy the story. It is an incredible feeling!

"The joy of creating and painting and reading your own book to your grandchildren
outweighs the frustration of sending it to publishers and receiving it back again with very
nice letters, but no contract! Just this year the youngest in the book, Lulu, (who is now at
school) suggested next time I visit she will be able to read Elf to me, which completes the
circle and is something every Granny should aim for! Mind you, the number of times I have
read Elf to her she probably knows it off by heart anyway!"

Outrageously energetic self publisher, Yvonne Blakeney, **Where's Elf?**, 2008

The Downside of Self Publishing:

Time Constraints

You can see from the activities above, you have gone from being a writer and an illustrator to a full-time distributor. You may no longer have time to produce your second book and the third and so on. Adding to this, you may have already a very full life, with commitments to a workplace and a home. Taking on the business which self publishing is not for the time-poor.

Self Driven

This probably says more about me than any other notes. I find it very easy to get distracted, because the deadlines I impose are exactly that – self-imposed! There are times when you need assistance and if you are a web researcher like I am, it doesn't take much to get distracted. The worst thing I did was sign up for the various newsletters from other publishers and booksellers in a bid to watch what was on offer in the market. I get distracted by the reviews and find I am very quickly making an order for a book via Fishpond. Aaaagghhhhhh! Subsequently, it doesn't take much to move the deadline to fit in with life. It would be lovely to have a support cast around you, nursing you through the process – and I am not talking about family and friends here! Unfortunately, when you are a self publisher, you do not have a team permanently in place. You are on your own.

Investment

The costs to produce an effective print run can be a barrier to entry. It is a toss-up – a glamorous five-star trip around the world, or a book? The outlay required for an offset printed book can be over $5,000.00 by the time you have organised the printing, delivery, distribution and marketing.

> Dan Kelly from Boolarong Press, Brisbane, spoke at a workshop in Toowoomba. He described the disheartening fact that many self publishers begin with zeal, picking up their first 1,000 copies and in a relatively short timeframe are left with hundreds of copies in boxes lining their garages. Their enthusiasm is dampened by the enormity of the task of selling enough books to break-even, let alone make a profit.

Multiple Roles

As a self publisher, you quickly discover that you must become a Jack (or Jill) of all trades. You are already a writer and an illustrator. How do you feel about also being an editor, a graphic designer, a publicist, a marketing guru, a distribution and warehousing agent, a booking agent for public speaking or school appearances – in other words, everything! The enormity of the task can be off-putting to some people.

Peer Recognition

Maybe I need to be researching human nature, because there seems to be an ingrained emotional hierarchy which says that recognition from friends and family (whilst wonderful) is not as important or as fulfilling for writers as receiving recognition from industry peers. To have your book published is to have your work validated. This is despite the fact there is no information available regarding the number of books which are remaindered (sold by the publisher at a reduced price), let alone information widely accessible on how many copies are sold in the first place.

The Reality

Conventional wisdom says you can sell fifty copies to your nearest and dearest without being too much of a pain in the neck. Most self published books sell around one to two-hundred copies. In a **Publishers Weekly** article *'Turning Bad Books into Big Bucks'*, it is noted that whilst the traditional publisher strategy is to achieve large volume sales of a limited number of books, self publishing companies aim to sell thousands of books by the hundred.

6. The eBook

Created in a digital format, eBooks are downloaded from websites to an eBook reader. For the consumer, the eBook reader can store a large number of books. For the publisher, it eliminates the cost of materials. The publishing and distribution platforms for eBook are relatively new and aggressively dynamic.

Offering a means for writers and readers to come together electronically with a degree of immediacy and for a much lower financial impost is one of the great advantages of this new publishing model. It is an advance on both the traditional model and the self publishing model, whereby there are still those who are gatekeepers of style. Now authors can have a greater input than ever before.

> John Birmingham, **He Died With a Felafel in His Hand**, uses POD and eBooks now as part of his writing 'strategy'. He takes a character out of one of his published books, follows their story for a while longer and shares this with readers via eBook.

To Pursue eBooks

The platforms for building eBooks are still jostling for number one in the market place and those producing eBooks now are at the whim of the outcome of the battle of the eBook readers. Think of the battle between VHS and... what was that other machine?!?!

There are so many different avenues available right now that facilitate the creation of eBooks. I did start writing a very prescriptive list for you, and then had an epiphany. It is such a fast moving area of publishing that it would be remiss of me if I didn't simply 'show' you in the right direction, rather than 'tell' you how to actually build an eBook!

Amazon, Lightning Source, Blurb, Google Books, Book.ish, Booku are just a few providers offering eBook construction and sales in the market, as I write. Yes, you did read the same names in POD. Each offer you the opportunity to create your own account and each have a 'how to' guide to lead you through the process. My advice to you is to take a moment to actually read the 'terms and conditions'. In each, you cannot progress with the account if you don't AGREE to the 'terms and conditions'.

Hands up any and all of you who have gone through the process of loading software onto your computer, simply clicked 'yes' to the 'terms and conditions' in a bid to hasten the process. Well, it is you I am genuinely appealing to. Without reading these 'terms and conditions', you might inadvertently hand over the copyright of your book, limit your territories where your book is available or jeopardise your right to distribute your book with other eBook promotional platforms.

> The latest way for self published writers of eBooks or hard copy versions to get their book in front of a reading audience is go to **www.writersweb.com.au**. A panel of passionate readers reviews the book and provides comments. Part of the book is viewable to whet the appetite of the purchaser-to-be, who (hopefully) then clicks the 'buy now' button.
>
> Based on the farmers' market model, emerging self published writers can connect direct to their readers and become authors in the process, **writers' web** is specifically for emerging Australian writers and Australian readers. It allows the reader to be the judge, the role traditionally taken by the publisher and is also a great way to 'get spotted' by mainstream publishers through the reader reviews and reader profiles on the site.

And where does this leave you?

You probably have that overwhelming sense of fatigue right now. The difficulty of the decision-making process is probably one very good reason why aspiring writers flock to writers festivals – hoping to glean even a modicum of insight into which road they should travel.

The best thing to do – is to start. So what if you start negotiating with a vanity publisher, then get stage fright, and send your manuscript to twenty conventional trade publishers. You then read about incredible self publishing success stories, like that of Australia's two highest selling authors, Matthew Reilly and Rachael Birmingham and then think 'I can do this too!' With a second (or third or fourth!) wind you will be inspired to make more inquiries.

Regardless – stick to some fundamentals, follow your gut instinct, and be true to yourself.

In the Words of a Child

"Publishing a book is a great feeling! When you see the book for the very first time you look at it and say 'Wow! I made this!' It feels wonderful to know that you did all the hard work and you achieved something as great as this!"

Emily, age 12, author & illustrator **Too Busy Lizzie** and **Lizzie in the Bush**, about having her books published.

13 **Build it**

The actual physical construction of the book is reliant on both computer and design skills.

There are three options to create your book as a digital, print-ready file.

1. Use a specialist company (such as Little Steps) which provides, to self publishing authors, services such as production and printing, design and illustration, editing and proofreading, ISBN registration and so on.
2. Use a professional graphic designer to set up the print-ready file.
3. Do it all yourself.

The remainder of this chapter is primarily intended to explain the process for those who elect to go it alone – and yes, you will have a sense of déjà vu when reading some sections!

Preparing the Book

Irrespective of what program you use to create your document, whether it is InDesign or Quark (for those who seem to have conquered the Mac and have technical prowess) or simply Microsoft Publisher (back to basics for me!) – creating a 'book' has been made possible by using the PDF (portable document format). This means the document has the images embedded, the font and formatting decisions are saved and it practically becomes tamper proof.

Half Title (Page 1)

It may not seem like much, but the Half Title is actually a very important page. This page is functional rather than informative in that it makes up the count for a thirty-two page picture book. It includes the title of the book and often a little vignette, which is like a 'teaser' or a sample of what is to come.

The general rule of thumb is to continue the font from the Front Cover through the Half Title and the Full Title pages. Differentiate the pages by full-size font on the Front Cover, approximately 50 per cent on the Full Title Page and 25 per cent on the Half Title Page.

Imprint Page (Page 2)

The Imprint Page is crucial. It is located often on the left-hand side of a double spread and contains all the information about the book which ensures that the book's copyright is allocated correctly, that the book is recorded and stored in the National Library of Australia correctly and that the author and publisher are acknowledged.

Typically the page will look like this:

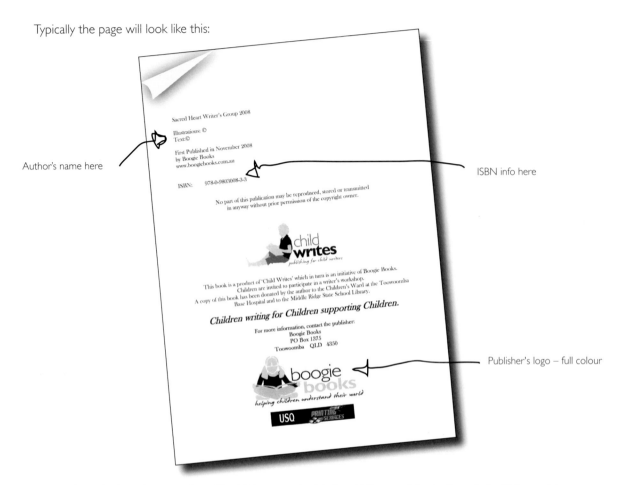

Author's name here

ISBN info here

Publisher's logo – full colour

It is useful to look at the notes for self publishers on the National Library of Australia website. This provides guidelines as to what information is essential and what is preferable. For example, it is essential to include the ISBN and the publisher's name. It is preferable to include contact information for the publisher. Look at the imprint page on published children's books for the information that can be included by virtue of personal choice. For example, the materials used to create the illustrations or if the paper is from renewable sources.

As a self publisher, it is useful for you to think about how you are going to brand yourself. This means the message you wish to impart on a regular, consistent basis. It may be in the form of a designed logo promoting your own publishing imprint, a business name or your own personal name. There is more about this in the marketing chapter.

Being 'published' means having material issued for sale or distribution to the public. There are publishing conventions in Australia, and indeed around the world, which support the documentation and recordkeeping for this material. As mentioned earlier, in Chapter 7, Plan it, the ISBN agency in Australia is Thorpe-Bowker.

The International Standard Book Number (ISBN), when allocated and then displayed on the imprint page, is one of the key differentiating points between published material and material which has simply been printed. With the ISBN comes a number of obligations for the publisher, such as sending copies of the books to the National Library of Australia and your state library. This is known as Legal Deposit. It is subsequently a courtesy requirement for you to send a copy to your local library.

"The allocation of an ISBN to a work automatically ensures its inclusion in the Australian Books in Print directory... the information is reproduced in international bibliographies such as Global Books in Print." **www.thorpe.com.au**

See, your book can be found if anyone is looking! But don't be lulled into a false sense of security by the wording 'automatically ensures its inclusion'. I think it should read 'automatically ensures eligibility of inclusion'. Not all the work is done for you. You still have to complete a form www.thorpe.com.au/forms/files/new_pub_entry.pdf to submit for your free listing in the directory.

Full Title (Page 3)

The Full Title sits beside the Imprint. The page usually includes the book's title (same font as Front Cover, though usually 50 per cent of the original size) the author's name and the publisher's logo. The design, as with all the other pages, is yours to determine.

Double Page Spreads

If you think of the pages being Half Title (page 1), Imprint (page 2), Full Title (page 3), then... (and are you concentrating?)

Pages four and then five begin as a double page spread, then pages six and seven and so on until page thirty-two. Really, you can now see a thirty-two page picture book is only twenty-nine pages of text and illustration. Furthermore, this means fourteen potential double spreads and one single spread at the end. Setting up the pages depends on the software you use. However, it can be as simple as 'viewing' the document as in two page view. If your illustrations line up and it looks as you want it to, then it is right.

End Papers

I really like the End Papers! Whilst end papers are traditionally a blank coloured piece of paper used in hardcover books to anchor the body of the book to the hard cover, I really enjoy the idea of making a decorative statement at the beginning and the end of the book. It is an opportunity to embellish the book a little more without distracting the reader. It also means ONE MORE page turn before the story starts. Nothing like the build-up of anticipation and, subsequently, the joy of delayed gratification!

Setting up these End Papers is as simple as inserting the illustrations on all the other pages. You would have already determined the design of the page in the dummy rough – whether or not you are using repetitive design elements, a new illustration or simply coloured squares. You can then choose which pages to add them to. I add them to the Inside Front Cover. Then on the opposite side, I reverse the image – think mirror. For the page which is the left-hand side to the Half Title, I revert back to the original design. Does that make sense? I have to say – it is a tough one to write about – you are better off muddling around actually trying it rather than rationalising it!

Front Cover

Now consider the following points which, I can tell you, I learned the hard way!

Clearly Visible Cover

The number one thing to remember is to make sure the title of the book is clearly visible from a distance! Imagine a potential reader walking into the bookstore or cruising around the internet looking for children's picture books. A resoundingly clear title will capture their eye immediately.

On my first book cover, **I Can Do Anything**, the title is at the bottom of the page. This meant there was a great deal of blank space above the illustration, with nothing more than a wash of colour. When it sat on forward facing shelves in bookstores, or some shelves which have a 'no-slip' barrier, you couldn't see anything other than the blank space. What a disaster! Eeeeekkkkkk!

Author and Illustrator Details

Whilst I can imagine that you are conceivably jumping out of your skin at the thought of your name being on the front of a real, seriously real, book – keep in mind that, as an unknown, this is not the information which will sell the book for you! You need the front cover of your book to be attractive compared to all the other books available on the market.

Amazing Cover Illustration

Your front cover illustration must be amazing! This is going to be the deal clincher – the one single thing that will make the purchaser want to pick up your book and not the one beside it. Then, and only then, will they flick through the pages and see if this is the story for them.

Here are two activities to help you gauge how eye-catching your cover is:

1. Do a mock up of your cover on heavy card, or consider (seriously) doing a number of trial covers. Take it (or them) to a bookstore (preferably one where they know you) and see how your covers compare. If you are feeling bold, slip them onto the shelf one at a time. For each one, see if it 'sits' well with the other titles. Does it look washed out and insignificant or does it demand your attention?

2. Show others. Ask a group of children from your local school their opinion about your cover, and which one they like the best. Then ask a group of parents. This is the 'glance test' used in the industry for reviewers and buyers.

> Did I tell you earlier that at Graeme Base's '*The Waterhole*' exhibition, he generously shared a number of his potential cover designs? There were many different versions of fonts, of basic layout and of different illustrations.

Back Cover

The back cover is just as important when looking at increasing the chances of selling your book. There are three aspects which can be included on the back cover.

Blurb

Consider adding a 'blurb' – an insight into the book. A blurb is a summary of the book. Don't give away everything though – leave the reader wondering. It is a teaser. You know yourself when you wander through the bookstore and pick up a book (because you like the cover) and then you flip the book over and read the back. If the teaser on the back actually makes you want to know more, then it is powerful enough to ensure you spend more time with the book – hopefully all the way to the checkout! Test your 'blurb' as well. Read it aloud to your friends, enemies and the lady at the cornerstore. You will get a truthful answer from the last two!

Review

You can add a review to your book cover. Show someone (particularly a well-known someone) a draft of your book and ask them to give you a written endorsement. Add this to the book cover, with the reviewer's details. There is something intrinsically powerful about a word-of-mouth recommendation.

Author Information

This is a great location for including information about you as the author and/or illustrator. You may include a photo, a brief biography or an illustrated self-portrait. If you are feeling a little uncomfortable about this, you can include this same information in the body of the book, either on the inside back cover or on the imprint page or on the half title – wherever you want!

Scan and Set

If you have decided to do everything yourself, you will need to create the digital file for your book. The simplest (and the most accessible) way to actually build your book involves a methodical process of scanning the original images, in order of their placement in the book. That is, scan the images and save them, then set up the file and import the images into the file in order – the illustration for the front cover being scanned first, the endpaper next, half title… and so on.

Talk about learning from my mistakes! The first illustrations I prepared for **Lily, Fabourama, Glamourama**, were A2 drawings. When I discovered that in order to scan them I would have to use a drum scanner, rather than a conventional copy shop scanner, AND I had to send them away to a capital city as there were no machines where I lived AND AND AND the possible cost was going to be hundreds of dollars… I had an enforced epiphany! I would re-do all the illustrations A3 size – the table size of most industrial sized flat bed scanners – and I did!

Scan the images as a JPEG file, not a PDF. (The former acronym is from Joint Photographic Experts Group, which doesn't really refer to what the file does – compresses the image without losing quality – but rather recognises the origin of the method. There you go – you learn something new every day!) Where was I? Oh, don't use PDF for saving scanned images. You can't manipulate them in any way, like cropping or colour mixing, and you may need to do this in the future.

There are two more things you need to know at this point – DPI and PPI. DPI (dots per inch) refers to how many dots of ink are dropped onto page to make an image. PPI (pixels per inch) refers to how many boxes of colour are on a screen to make an image.

You don't need to scan the image at the same resolution that you will be using to print the image. A print-quality image is 600 DPI, but scan the image at a third, so 200 DPI. Any higher and you will have HUGE files. And if you are considering an eBook, the DPI needs to be significantly smaller to facilitate the page loading in a timely manner!

When I am saving a finished book file, the ones destined for the printer are saved as PDF for 'high quality printing' and are 1200DPI. The Child Writes books which are included in the Jetstar Inflight Entertainment offering are saved as 'screen quality' and are 96DPI.

Now, don't scream and shout at me – I am the world's laziest pseudo-graphic designer after all – but I do use Microsoft Publisher to set up my own books. It is also the software I used to set up the plethora of books produced so far with the Child Writes Program. I know, I know, I know – NOBODY in the 'industry' uses anything so unstable or as inflexible. And yes, I know, I know, I know – the design constraints make it practically unusable for anyone else.

My only caveat is that it has worked because the Child Writes students are organised. They have solved all the design problems in the dummy rough, know exactly where the text is to be placed and have accepted the construction of the half and full title pages, the cover and back cover and the imprint page. Collecting all these files into one bundle, or rather, one publisher file actually works.

So how do you 'talk' to the printers? The solution – PDF! You can translate Publisher files into a PDF for printing. The Portable Document Format has been around since 1993. By saving a file as a PDF, you are able to have a file that cannot be corrupted or changed by any other party. In the new world of digital printing, you can take your USB to the printer.

Regardless of the program, you will simply save the finished document as a PDF.

Visiting Your Printer

I have worked with Tony at USQ Printing Services with all of the Child Writes books to date, including slowly rebuilding the books written in the first years of the program. Sometimes, the words from those 'in the know' are more useful than my raving!

My name is Tony and I work in the Prepress Department at USQ Printing Services. My primary role is to examine supplied artwork, such as the PDF file Emma has helped you create over the last few chapters, and ensure it will proceed through our workflow to finished print stage.

The benefit of PDF compared to receiving native files, fonts and links (like we used to in the past) is that the PDF contains everything required to print your job. Fonts are embedded, images are optimised, and the PDF format can even describe things as the colour space to print in, etc.

PDF is a wonderful file format. It lets you hand your project off to us as one final file that contains all of the elements necessary to produce a quality printed piece. But just because a file is in PDF format does not automatically mean that it is suitable for high quality printing! PDFs can be optimised for printing, on-screen viewing, or even interactive purposes. So keep in mind if you are generating a PDF that is intended for high quality print you should stick to the Press Optimised defaults if your software package has options for them.

All of the PDFs we receive at USQ Printing Services go through a pre-flight procedure as part of our workflow. So even if you are not sure about the quality of the PDF you are generating, our workflow will analyse the file and alert us to potential problems. Here is a brief overview of the main points we look for when checking supplied PDFs:

- *Fonts are embedded. This will ensure that your carefully set type will not be substituted with default fonts at print time.*

• *Images are high resolution. When it comes to printing we want the highest quality images available. Your file size will increase to include all of this detail but the end result will look a lot better than printing low-resolution images that were intended for on-screen purposes.*

• *Page counts are correct and trim size is defined. Keep in mind that for a saddle stitched book you need to work in multiples of four. Also your original document should be created at the final trim size for your printed piece.*

The pre-flight procedure performs quite a number of other technical checks but if these main points are met we can generally produce a quality printed product for you. If there are any issues with your file we would notify you at this stage and discuss how we can work around these. Otherwise it's onto to proof stage where we print off one copy of your job for a final check. Then once you have signed off on the proof, the presses can start rolling!

One final point. Although I have given you a quick overview of things to check for when creating PDFs it's always a good idea to speak with your print provider at the start of any project. They may have other specific requirements for their own particular production methods and if you can get this information up-front it can help reduce potential headaches further down the production line.

I hope you have found this brief guide helpful... Happy writing!

In the Words of a Child

"In primary school, the teachers always told us nursery rhymes. I have forgotten most of them but I have always remembered the story about how the cow jumped over the moon. When I got a chance of making my own picture book I was so excited but I didn't have an idea for my book. I'm bad at making up stories so I wanted to find a story and build up on it. When I was trying to thinking of some ideas, Emma told our group that we could write about something we saw or an experience that was funny. I thought about that and it actually helped me. I remembered when I was in grade three, I was reading this story that was about a group of children making jokes about the nursery rhyme, **The Cow Jumped Over the Moon**. I was thinking about the story and I suddenly came up with so many ideas, so **The Cow That Jumped Over the Moon** became the title for my book."

Yonghui, age 10, author & illustrator **The Cow That Jumped Over the Moon**, about the title.

|4 **Print it**

You are in a fabulous position. In your hand is a USB stick with a file saved as a PDF – your book. I don't want to drive you insane by saying there are tonnes of options, but the world is now your oyster!

Rather, we will concentrate on the immediate options for getting a book into your hot little hands.

Inevitably, the matter of cost arises at some point. After all, you've poured yourself into writing and illustrating and you are busting to see the book in print! There are a number of considerations which directly impact on the pricing of your project:

- The printing option you choose
- The quantity you choose to print
- The binding method
- The paper stock

Just so you know right now – we believe full-colour should be non-negotiable for children's picture books!

The decision making process will be greatly aided if you can answer the following:

- What is the purpose and scope of your book? Is it for a gift, or are you hoping it will become the next bestseller?
- What is your willingness and ability to market? Do you have the confidence, skills and time to market your book?
- What storage space do you have available (if offset / large print run chosen)?
- And finally, what is your budget?

Printing Options

Digital Printing

Beyond what your little printer can do at home, commercial digital printing is about handling heavier paper and larger volumes. It is considered 'quick' printing and is perfect for short print runs. Order a quantity and then store the books until sold. The paper is sheet-fed through the printing machine and this paper is as close to pre-purchased finished size as possible. If you stray from the predetermined sizes, the paper is simply cut and discarded. You pay for the entire sheet of paper, regardless of the trim.

Offset Printing

This option is predominantly used for larger print runs. Whilst the same offer of high-quality finish can be made, it is used to achieve economies of scale. That is, the expense of setting up the book is shared over the number of books printed. This means that the per unit cost is reduced, the more copies you print.

Inventory management is required. The paper is roll-fed through the printing machine and then folded and cut to finished size.

Binding is the process of securing loose pieces of paper and making sure they stay together with the cover. There are a number of different binding options available.

Binding Options

Saddle Stitch

Staples are used down the middle of a folded sheet of paper. It is a very resilient method of binding, especially for children's books. It is the method of binding used for the Child Writes A4 digitally printed books.

Perfect Bind

Otherwise known as thermal binding. In perfect binding, tape or plastic strips are fused to the paper using heat and glue. This means that the book can be laid out flat. It can be used for offset printed books or for digitally printed books where there are not any signatures. A signature is a bundle of sixteen pages which are then sewn together.

Case Bind

The pages, regardless of how they are printed, are arranged in signatures and sewn together, and hard covers are attached. The endpapers form part of the signature and one side is glued to the cover. It is possibly the most attractive and there is something about the validity of a hardbound book. It is the most expensive binding. We probably know the case binding as a hardcover book.

Spiral Bind

This is otherwise known as comb binding. It is commonly used in recipe books, allowing for the pages to stay flat, without being pressed to remain there or anchored in any way. The pages are independent of each other. It is the most robust binding, yet it doesn't allow double spread illustrations to butt up together.

Paper Options

Your printer should have a paper fan deck – similar to those of a colour chart – with the different paper they can source for your book. The difference in the paper types can be related to the thickness, colour and finish of the paper.

Most book papers are off-white or low white and they are opaque, so you can't see through to the text on the other side. Typically, the paper for the guts of the book is light, measured by g/m^2 (or gsm – grams per square metre). The lighter the g/m^2, the thinner the paper. A good weight for a picture book is a resilient $100g/m^2$. A gloss finish makes the illustrations shine on the page and is a little easier to clean marks left by little fingers!

Paper stock for the cover should be much heavier, anything from 120 to 200 g/m^2, even as heavy as 350 gsm. A cello cover – literally a piece of cellophane – acts as a barrier much as contact did to those text books you had when you were younger! Gloss is more hardwearing, but again it depends on the finish you are looking for to complement your book.

Book Size Options

The size of the book is entirely up to you.

It sounds very trite to say it like that, even a little dismissive, but the book size IS really entirely up to you. As mentioned in the section about the dummy rough, you will have made this decision after researching what sizes of books are on the market, talking to booksellers to see what they prefer to handle, and visiting the post office to see what the postage costs could possibly be.

When Yvonne Blakeney finished her first book, all her illustrations were completed on A4 paper. This sounds reasonable, until I tell you they were horizontal, not portrait. This decision did affect her book and her printing options considerably. Horizontal A4 could not be digitally printed at USQ Printing Services, unless it was spiral bound. This wasn't the plan and Yvonne had to be incredibly flexible to change her perceptions of what her finished book would look like.

Incidentally, the book which I set up for her won a printing prize for USQ Printing Services from NIPPA (the Network of In-house Print Professionals Australasia Inc).

Sorry! I couldn't help but include this!

Cost Comparison

All of these decisions directly influence the cost of the printing.

As a cost comparison, let's look at the following scenario. So that we are comparing 'apples with apples', I will assume the print order is, in its simplest:

- An A4 sized full colour children's picture book
- Thiry-six pages inner on full gloss A3 paper stock, 100 gsm white bond
- Cover – 120 gsm paper with cello glazing
- Saddle stitch binding

In a bid to share some 'real life' information, I organised for a quote for the book described above, with the following result.

Offset Printing: for 1,000 copies, cost is approximately $3.70 per copy.
Digital Printing: for a single copy, cost is approximately $14.15 per copy.

The differences are huge and the final decision will be entirely yours. Read beyond this point for information about sharing the book and about marketing options. You will be able to gauge how active you are prepared to be to leverage sales in a very crowded marketplace.

For the children who participate in the Child Writes program, we routinely digitally print ten copies of each book. This equates to a total printing cost of only $150. Remember, the product is not currently tested commercially, so there is no need to establish a realistic sell price.

Basically, if you are giving your book away as a gift, consider small digital print runs. It is practically a print on demand mentality. If you are intending to make a business out of your book, print the books via offset. This will ensure you have enough room to facilitate bringing other people into the process if you need to (distributors, booksellers etc).

Choosing the Printer

Personal recommendation from others is again the best way to find a printer. When you are looking at the books in the stores, have a look at who the printer is. You will know which ones you like. When you narrow down your search, do some homework. Use the internet to find out about their product offering. Ask:

- Can they do most of the finishing in-house or is it outsourced (therefore adding time and extra handling costs)?
- What volume can they handle within what timeframe?
- How many colour proofs are allowed for in the initial quote?
- If there are changes to be made, do you have to resubmit the PDF file or can they make the changes?
- And a good one – do you feel as though they think your print job is the most important thing in the world?

Don't let geography be a hindrance in deciding on a printer. After all, most Australian publishers get their books printed overseas. For example, Red Planet Printing (an agency in Australia) work with a number of printers in China and has a very well constructed set of print guidelines to follow. With file sharing sites such as **www.share-it.com.au** which use the internet and file compression programmes (so you can send large files to the printers, rather than physically delivering a USB stick), it is entirely manageable.

Again – geography is not a problem. The first Child Writes eBook was produced in Sydney by Rogue Studios and all the files (proofs included), were sent via email. One of my students is from India and went home for the summer holidays – taking with her a USB stick with her PDF printready picture book to get a quote from a local printer!

The Mock Book (or Galley)

This is a really useful tool. Have you ever wondered how a book can be on the bookshelf, ready for sale, yet it has reviews and thoughts and recommendations from people the author may or may not even have met? In actuality, what happens is that the book has been written and illustrated and edited and proofread and polished – and then a mock book is produced. If the pages are bound with a full-colour cover, sometimes these books are called Advanced Reading Copies.

> I originally believed 'reviews' were only the entitlement of authors who had a second print-run, so these reviews could be included at this time. It is scary to 'fess up to such naivety at times…

The world of digital printing means you can do a 'print run' of ten copies for around $15.00 per book. You can then send the galley to a host of influencers in the product purchase cycle. These include book reviewers who work for newspapers and magazines like the **Australian Woman's Weekly** *Great Reads*, book clubs like ABC television's *First Tuesday Book Club* and journals such as the **Australian Literary Review**.

Also consider the more relevant organisations which are directly associated with your book, even if you have to think a little outside the square. For example, if you have written about native Australian animals, why not contact **Australian Geographic**? If you have written about a child being scared of bumps in the night, contact the **Australian Psychology Association**? One more example is straight from the front cover of Peter Carnavas' book **Jessica's Box…** '*Shortlisted book of the Year 2009 – Speech Pathology Australia*'.

I would suggest going through the same lovely process you went through when looking for a publisher. Go to your favourite bookstore or library and read the reviews in publications and take note of who wrote the review. Now you can send the book directly to a person, rather than a generic 'Dear Sir/Madam'. Another option is to seek an endorsement from someone who already has an established name, such as a celebrity or a well-known author.

Imagine the impact if you wrote a book about a little girl's cooking adventure and it was endorsed by the 2010 Junior Master Chef, Isabella. What do you do with those glorious reviews? Why, include them on the cover if they are fabulous and start those printing presses!

You have it in your hand, and you are ready to go. Now let's recoup some of those printing costs…

In the Words of a Child

"I couldn't believe it when I saw the book, my very own book – finished, printed, bound – when it came back from the printers. I didn't really believe I had written and illustrated a real book until then."

Annabel, age 11, author & illustrator **The Tea Party Terror**, about printing her book.

15 **Market it**

To market-to-market to buy a fat... book!

The consumer world is so sophisticated now, yet the goal for merchants remains the same as it has for time immemorial – to sell what is produced. In order to sell something, you need to find the buyer. When the world was a simpler place, geographical considerations meant the majority of trade was conducted where people actually lived.

Now we really do live in a global community. The consumer can order a book online via Australian online bookstore Fishpond and it may be sourced from the UK, but it will be sent from the USA. The process is practically automated and the consumer doesn't even have to give the supply chain a second thought. There are thousands of new titles each week to choose from. The most pertinent question is: how does the consumer know which book to order?

Of course, in a perfect marketing world, the goal is to produce something needed, something which solves a problem, therefore it WILL sell. Whilst you may believe your book offers solutions to a problem – entertaining a bored soul, being bullied at school, dealing with death – books are still in a product category where you have to convince the buying public your book is needed in their world.

It is up to you! It is amazing how much you can do to ensure your book reaches its target destination – into the hands of wonderful parents, carers and teachers, who are all willing to share your words with their children.

There are three areas you need to be able to describe – yourself, as the author; the book, as the product; and the target market, as the reader. There is a matrix which can, at a glance, provide a summary for you to then underpin any marketing plan – The SWOT Analysis.

SWOT Yourself

First, let's do a little self analysis. Yes, you are going to see what tools and skills you already have and how to mop up if you identify any weaknesses. You need to understand how your immediate world impacts on any future strategies you may make as you commit to what is the business of self publishing.

That leads us to a SWOT analysis – yep, you're going to SWOT yourself, your book and the target market! Waahhhhh? I hear you yell like Old Aunty Ay Ya down the road! Don't ignore me now and close the book. A SWOT analysis is incredibly easy and simple and inexpensive to do. And it will save you a tonne of time in the future.

A SWOT analysis is a marketing tool, where an analysis of an organisation or product is done by considering its strengths and weakness, and the opportunities and threats in the marketplace. By using a simple matrix, you can see on one page how the product (your book) will function outside of the comfort of your studio. This will ensure you have all the information you need to start a marketing campaign.

Below are examples of what facets you can investigate. The list is by no means exhaustive but merely a guide to get you started.

Strengths and Weaknesses

Strengths and weaknesses are within you and they are tangible and identifiable, so you can influence, utilise, diminish or control them.

Answer the following questions, keeping in mind:

That which is driven by you ensuring you reach your goal is a STRENGTH, and that which jeopardises you goal is a WEAKNESS.

Regarding strengths and weaknesses, how would you respond (either positively or negatively), when I ask you about your:

- Writing skills
- Illustrating skills
- Computer skills
- Marketing skills
- Personality
- Personal attributes
- Organisational abilities
- Manuscript
- Financial capacity

Opportunities and Threats

Opportunities and threats happen around you in your environment and you need to be aware, prepared and organised to take advantage of, or diminish their impact.

That which is external to you — your home, your relationships, the marketplace — are areas posing OPPORTUNITIES or THREATS.

Regarding opportunities and threats, this is what is happening out there.

- Saturated marketplace for genre
- Niche subject matter for a story
- Limited marketing budget
- Unwillingness of distributors to take on single titles
- Support: emotional, physical, financial or mental (or lack thereof)
- Increased printing, paper and distribution costs
- Access to a supportive community — internet, personally, professionally

SWOT yourself as the author. If you like, start by writing a list, the first draft of what could become your curriculum vitae. It can include a list of the courses you have attended, significant jobs you have held, and writing successes you have had. The better understanding you have of your attributes, the more 'sell' points you will uncover. Then, consider your strengths and weaknesses. Begin adding them to the matrix.

SWOT your product, your book. Describe your book in more depth than just the blurb on the back cover. Again, this is in a bid to uncover some more 'sell' points that will help you later as you develop your marketing plan. The book's description can include the genesis of the idea, the names of your supporters, the process by which you wrote and illustrated it. It is also important to consider what other books are out there in competition with your book and to try to communicate your 'point of difference'.

And finally, SWOT your target market, your reader. There is no escaping it – you have to know who your target market is. The target market can be described in terms of the attributes that make a group a 'group'. The descriptors are initially demographics, like gender, age, income and location. It is particularly useful if you can define your market in more detail, including descriptors nominating emotional responses (for example, point-of-sale impulse), purchase habits (routine or not) and purchase motivation (regular, impulse or seasonal).

The first step to indentifying your target market is to research, research, research! You want to know who might be interested in your book. You want to know who else is appealing to the same buyers. (You have already been doing this research along the various stages in the book-making process. Remember, you have been to the bookstore and had a look at publishers supporting similar books.)

SWOT Pro Forma

Strengths	Weaknesses
Opportunities	**Threats**

Using it

As you look at the matrix, consider the centre of the lines as representing you. If something is a great threat, make note of it close to the cross hairs. If it is a remote opportunity, make mention of it on the perimeter of the matrix. An example could be:

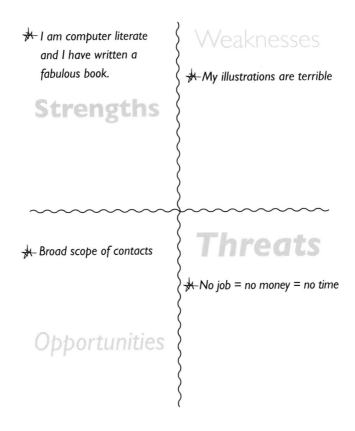

Analyse it

Use the information that has evolved from the above analysis to specifically determine the facets of a promotional plan that will work best for you.

Miss Great Example:

Strengths

- I am computer literate and love Twitter and Facebook, as I keep up with my past students.
- I am a teacher librarian working within a school population of 1,200 students.

- I have worked in this environment for ten years, having personally taught 2,000 students.
- I am recognised within the industry as a master teacher.
- My 'How to teach children how to read' is finished.

Weaknesses

- My illustrations are terrible.
- I can't bear standing talking to a group of adults – much happier with children.
- I run out of energy quickly.

Opportunities

- There has never been a better time in publishing history for self-publishing.
- I am still in touch with all my students and their parents.
- Interest in literacy is increasing.

Threats

- I am one of half-a-million others this year alone attempting to achieve the same goal – to see my name in print.
- I don't have any financial support. Therefore I can't take on self publishing as a full-time commitment.

Now what do you do with the information? You devise strategies to exploit your strengths to create opportunities, and you work on converting weaknesses into strengths, and threats into opportunities.

For Miss Great Example:

- Develop an online shop for own book, with limited print run. Maybe only a handful of collector's copies, signed, with personal notes, after a bidding war preprint!
- Given propensity to avoid crowds of adults, avoid committing to speaking arrangements at conferences or any author talks. However, organise school visits with students or author visits to libraries, as a 'resident' for a longer period of time, daytime hours only.
- As a confident writer, get a friend to take photos and then create own press releases to distribute.
- Commission children to input some illustrations, especially clever Johnny Blogs from 9B, or talented university students. Alternatively, contract an established illustrator.
- Develop an author website and use social media for marketing purposes.
- Research shows increasing interest in literacy. Develop a program. Contact schools or government departments.

You have made inroads into understanding the world around you and what you have to offer. By looking into these all in more detail, we can better assist you in gaining an insight into what will become your own marketing plan.

Target Market

First, as we mentioned, you have to know who your target market is. The target market can be described by the attributes which define that group. The descriptors are initially demographics, like gender, age, income and location. It is particularly useful if you can define your market in more detail, including descriptors which nominate emotional responses (for example, point-of-sale impulse), purchase habits (routine or not) and purchase motivation (regular, impulse or seasonal). Now you can understand why research-gathering tools under the guise of loyalty programs are so critical to a business.

It is not enough to say the target market for a children's picture book is children. Children are not driving the purchase decision. The target market, for example, for a children's picture book about wombats and their habitat could be women, aged between twenty-four and forty, who believe in supporting development in child literacy as well as a sustainable environment.

All of these descriptions help you FIND the buyers.

Research

The first step is research, research, research! If you spend some time researching who will be interested in your book and researching who else is appealing to the same buyers, it will certainly help point you in the right direction as far as spending your time, energy and money when you are promoting and distributing it. You have already been doing research along the various stages in the bookmaking process. Remember, you have been to the bookstore and had a look at publishers supporting similar books. Look for hints and suggestions for what to research. Debbie Higgs at Palmer Higgs has the completely awesome **'Self Publishers Guide'** available as an eBook from **www.palmerhiggs.com.au**. It contains excellent activities for identifying your target market and reaching them.

One of my favourite research moments is passively observing who is purchasing books. I go to a bookstore which has a coffee shop (so it doesn't look weird to be lingering) and I simply record my guesstimate regarding the physical demographics of the book. You can actively research genre sales to see if you are on the right track. Go to **www.bowker.com** for statistical data regarding genre sales and forecast genre sales.

Identify

Remember, you are a writer, so writing a description of who the book is targeted towards after you have completed your research should be manageable.

If you have written a book about a little girl with bad manners, and you realise that books focusing, for example, on manners are virtually non-existent in the current market, you may wish to strongly identify with this by rewriting your blurb for the back of your book OR setting up your promotional material to link with this.

If you identify your target purchaser, it makes finding them easier. As an example, the book about manners would possibly be relevant to parents with children about to start school, so advertising as a 'pre-school must-have' would be an appropriate way to communicate.

All promotional strategies hang on your identification of the target market, so spend a little time doing so.

The Four P's

The activities defining 'marketing' fit into four main considerations: Product, Price, Promotion and Place (distribution).

> In my first year at university, I was so bamboozled by the combination of exam pressure and the complete lack of parental pressure, that I failed the subject *Introduction to Marketing* – because I forgot one of the four 'P's' (can you believe I am telling you this?). Of course, with the degree well and truly completed now and a little life experience, you realise it is impossible in working practice to forget any element. If you do, the process of delivering what you have created to the end-user is unfeasible!
>
> Now, where was I…? **P**roduct, **P**rice, **P**romotion, **P**lace.

Product

You already have (or are close to having) your product – a hard or soft-covered full-colour children's picture book, written and (probably also) illustrated by you! It has been printed, by the boxful via offset printing or by the handful via digital printing. You have worked really hard to ensure the product is of the highest possible quality and you have made sure you have all the 'professional' touches, like ISBNs, logos and book design considered.

Develop Your Branding

A brand is a prescribed, consistent message delivered to the purchaser. It is all about deciding what you want to say and sticking to the message.

Branding a self published children's book depends on:

- The consistent use of the name and logo used for the publishing imprint
- The consistent use of that same logo on your website and in supporting marketing and administrative materials (such as business cards, press releases, e-mail signatures or order forms)
- The consistent use of colour, fonts and style across all marketing and administrative elements, a name reflecting who you (or your publishing imprint) are and what you do, and so on…

In fact, it is certainly worth developing your own 'style file'. This is a list of all the ways you communicate the promotional products you are using now or may use in the future. I didn't do this in the beginning. Rather, my branding has evolved as my level of involvement in this industry has increased. It is, however, easier to accomplish when it is planned beforehand.

You must be sure that you are communicating something consistent about yourself and your product, and that you are also connecting with your potential readers (remember that target market) on a level that they can understand and appreciate. There must be relevance. If you are creating a branding as a publishing imprint for children's books, use the bright and playful colours and style that will 'match' children's books, not a sterile or overly business-like logo which could suit a medical business or Fortune 500 company. Do the same with choosing an imprint or business name. What do you want it to communicate? Thurston Enterprises is not a good 'fit' for a publisher of children's book. However, names such as 'Little Steps', or 'Koala Books' are.

Spend some time looking at the branding of existing children's publishers, through the imprints and logos in their books, and the branding across their websites. Learn from them. Notice their names, logos and how they carry the colours, styles and fonts through. This is a sign of professionalism.

You don't have to develop a branding but if you do, it may create a sense of professionalism around your work that is not possible without it. There tends to be a stigma about self published books, that perhaps they are not as good because they 'couldn't' gain commercial publication. And traditionally there has been some merit to this stigma, as self publishers haven't always utilised the skills and tools to create products and businesses that were comparable in quality to their commercial counterparts. This quandary is fascinating as it is the complete opposite to the music industry – where the grungier more home-produced and self-promoted, the better. Go figure!

Fortunately, the tools available to self publishers have come a long way. You have chosen the route of self publishing for its many benefits, and you have a quality product in your hands (or on the way). Now you need to communicate that you are a professional publisher too. If you do that, your book won't stand out and scream "self published!"... and in fact, it will be difficult to tell the difference between it and a commercially published book – just as it should be.

You are creative. You can do this. Just like writing and illustrating, how you create your 'brand' is entirely up to you.

Branding Yourself

As you prepare to launch your book onto the unsuspecting public, give yourself an edit and a polish as well. Have a 'headshot' taken by a professional photographer (or a friend with a very, very good camera). Don't kid yourself into the glamour shot if you are not glamorous; there are countless stories from authors and illustrators out there who have disappointed their audiences when they don't look as young or as fabulous as they do in their publicity shot.

The photo can be used every time you introduce yourself. So far I have sent mine to be used as a conference introduction, a magazine column flag and to a capital city library for a summer reading program brochure, as well as using it on my curriculum vitae (CV) of course. You can do the same.

An author who uses her publicity photograph very effectively is Aleesah Darlison. Once she emerged as a published author, her face seemed to pop up everywhere – promoting conferences she was speaking at, in industry newsletters and groups to highlight her books and workshops... always the same professional photograph. The consistency made her seem 'known' and trustworthy very quickly. Check it out at **www.aleesahdarlison.com**. If you are in any way involved in the writing industry, you may have already seen her face around somewhere!

Branding Your Book

You want to get your book, or the image of your book, in front of as many eyes as possible. To accomplish that, you may choose to print additional material that will support the branding of your book. For example, you may print business cards with your contact information on the front, and a thumbnail image of the front cover of your book on the back. Carry these around everywhere. You might also consider postcards, bookmarks (useful gifts at school author talks), badges, stickers or flyers. Add a thumbnail of your book to the bottom of every outgoing email through your email signature.

You may also choose to produce supporting materials for your book to be used for author talks, library visits, website downloads and more. These may include fact sheets, colouring in pages, crosswords, find-a-word puzzles and other activities directly related to your story and its characters (if you've contracted an illustrator, you may need to request their help with this).

Consistency is the key. Whether you are creating promotional material or worksheets or presentations, keep the branding relevant, consistent and therefore, 'strong'.

Price

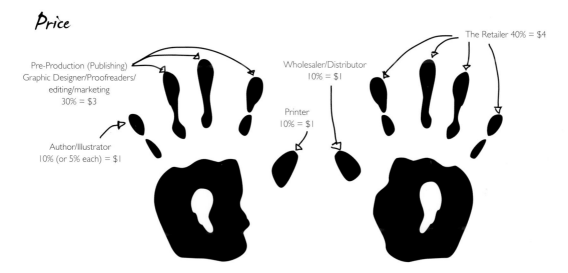

The Retailer 40% = $4

Pre-Production (Publishing) Graphic Designer/Proofreaders/ editing/marketing 30% = $3

Wholesaler/Distributor 10% = $1

Printer 10% = $1

Author/Illustrator 10% (or 5% each) = $1

Recommended Retail Price

Make sure that the RRP (recommended retail price) is the same, regardless of who is selling or where you are selling your book. Not many stores would be very impressed if they realised you were selling your book via your own website for a discount, nor does a customer want to pay more by purchasing through a particular channel rather than the other. Setting the RRP is arbitrary and is entirely your responsibility. I will abstain from an economics lecture, but suffice it to say, you cannot sell it for less than it costs to produce and you are selling to an educated marketplace, so the product must be cost comparable.

With your book in hand (if already printed), go to your favourite bookstore and make comparisons with other books in the market. Those books you are looking at have already been through the rigours of the publishing industry and deserve to be there. How do they compare? How does the product being offered at the same price point compare? Make sure you also talk to the booksellers. They, after all, spend a great deal of time talking to the end user – the customer! They will be able to quickly appraise your book in relation to the price you are proposing to sell it for.

Break Even Point

You must determine how many books you need to sell just to cover your printing costs. This is your break even point at its most basic. For example, if you print 1,000 books for $3.70 each, then you will have to sell 247 books at $14.95 to get your money back. That is just the printing!

"Keeping in mind the costs of selling a book: freight, storage, retailer discounts and the cost of returns, marketing and so on. A professional publisher would allow around 67 per cent of the RRP for all these costs."
Catharine Retter, Chairman of The Australian Book Group.

Let's make a little more money! Using this formula, for a RRP of $24.95, just over $16.70 will be your associated costs and if you add the printing, $20.40 will be absorbed, swallowed up, disintegrated by costs. You are left with $4.55, or just less than 18 per cent of the RRP.

Pay For Your Own Books

A great discipline is to 'pay' for the books you 'give' away for promotional purposes (such as sending away to be reviewed or as prizes for competitions). Literally, have a jar and put in $14.95 every time you give away a book. It will make you discerning, accountable and it will keep you on target to sell the 247 and reach your break-even point quickly. After this point, as the saying goes, it really is money for jam and all you have to spend is more of your time.

The great thing about working on a promotional plan and knowing that you are considering the distribution as well, is that you can use all of this information to develop a profitability model. Like working on the style file, spend some time manipulating the numbers to see what you can afford to pursue.

Place

How do you get your book from the box on your garage floor into the hands of your readers? There are a number of distribution channels to consider including the physical bookstore and the role of distributors, online bookstores and libraries.

Traditional Bookstores

When I started writing this a couple of years ago, it was a well-known fact that 80 per cent of book purchases happened at the store front, where a happy and relaxed book buyer is browsing and is attracted to pick up the book because of the cover. They then read the blurb on the back and maybe flick through the pages. If they are captured, they will read the book on the spot! You have a guaranteed sale, and if they love it, they will want to share this with others. Free word-of-mouth advertising! Now, only minutes later, it is a given that the same percentage of readers get book information online.

Getting into a physical bookstore is a tricky objective, mainly because even independent stores are loath to work with single titles. The workload involved in managing accounts for single titles is considered to outweigh the income which may be generated from the sale of the title. However, on the other hand, you may have better chances doing this with independent bookstores because they have greater decision-making power.

A SIDE THOUGHT...
Don't Ever Let the 'Single Title' Tag Deter You:

For a moment, you are Mathew Reilly or Rachael Birmingham and Kim McCosker… Look up their names via a Google search. They would have to be amongst the most successful Australian self published authors of our day…

So how do you get in the door? Load up your car with a couple of boxes and drive to the shop, walk in with an invoice book in hand and ask if they would consider stocking your book on consignment. Offer to manage the inventory on a regular basis and only charge back when sales have been made. You will, of course, not fail to mention you are doing a radio interview with the local radio station the following week and you have already organised a press release for the local newspaper. Oh, yes, and don't forget to mention you would be also delighted to be on-hand for an author event and book-signing.

Please note that bookstores will expect a commission of about 40 to 45 per cent on the RRP of each book sold through them.

Distributors

If you find it difficult or impossible to deal with bookstores directly due to their unwillingness to take on single titles, finding a distributor to take on your title may be the answer. Distributors take books from many independent authors and sell to bookstores and retail outlets on their behalf.

So, how do you find a distributor? Don't forget the magical tool, the internet. Rather than doing a broad Google search, such as 'children's book distributors', go straight to the Australian Publishers Association site, at **www.publishers.asn.au**. You will find a list of Australian and overseas distributors. Most sensibly, the listings include information as to whether or not they will consider single titles. Very useful!

Given the work involved in warehousing and distributing books, whether to stores or directly to book buyers, you have to keep in mind right now that distributors take about 60 per cent of the RRP.

The website **www.writersweb.com.au** is the latest way for self published writers of eBooks or hard copy versions to get their book in front of a reading audience. A panel of passionate readers reviews the book and provides comments. Part of the book is viewable to whet the appetite of the purchaser-to-be, who (hopefully) then clicks the 'buy now' button.

Based on the farmers' market model, emerging self published writers can connect direct to their readers and become authors in the process, **writers' web** is specifically for emerging Australian writers and

Australian readers. It allows the reader to be the judge, the role traditionally taken by the publisher and is also a great way to 'get spotted' by mainstream publishers through the reader reviews and reader profiles on the site.

Online Bookstores

Getting into the online bookstores is a relatively simple goal to attain. Nearly all eBook platforms offer an entry into their own online bookstore. This vertical integration means they can have a larger product offering and makes them focus on selling their brand, rather than your book. To sell your book in these behemoths, you still need to have a good cover, great reviews, excellent blurb, all the functionalities of a physical book.

Amazon

There are more than 30 million titles available on Amazon! It is an unbelievably formidable bookstore and I can genuinely understand why booksellers (you) aim for this as a promotion and distribution vehicle. But there are more than 30 million titles! Make sure you create an entry in Author Central, submitting your profiles, biography, book covers, and so on. As with all web profiles, update it regularly. You can use CreateSpace to organise POD product, you can upload a Kindle book, sell through Amazon Advantage and sign up for Search Inside, select word searches for the guts of your book, not just the title. It is a comprehensive offering and worth exploring. Each of these options is fully explained on the website. It is just that there are *more than* 30 million titles already on the shelf, so you need to do much more promotional work outside of Amazon, to lead consumers to seek out your title.

Fishpond

How about Fishpond – Australasia's biggest online store (it is based in Sydney). Whilst thousands and thousands of titles are available, there are options for self-publishers. You can list your book in the 'Sell Yours' section on the Book Products page. Or you can add to the Fishpond catalogue by adding your book first to the Nielsen Bookdata Database (email your book's ISBN to support@nielsenbookdata.com.au). Actually, while you are there, list your bibliographic details on this database as well. It is also free.

Other Online Bookstores

If you have self-published through a printer or publisher who offers some self-publishing services (such as Little Steps or Palmer-Higgs), you may find that they offer their own online bookstore through which your title can also be promoted. The advantage of this is that Palmer-Higgs Books OnLine is non-exclusive, therefore you can use it as your primary method of distribution or as an adjunct to other distribution methods you have put in place.

Your Own Website Store

Setting up your own website and online bookstore is very useful. It can be constructed by adding an e-commerce function to your already set up website or blog site. Keep in mind you will have to manage the 'warehouse' inventory and be responsible for postage and handling. It is important to have automatically generated 'reply' messages acknowledging an order and possibly a tracking mechanism so you can update your customer as to the status of their order. In this modern world of 'add to cart', consumers are already very sophisticated and won't tolerate anything less than this. Keep in mind though, if you have an online store, you still need promotion to drive your customers to the site.

Libraries

If you would like your book to be picked up by libraries, there are two strategies. The leg work for the first strategy is actually already done for you. Remember when we were walking you through the ISBN process, I made mention of the registration process you need to follow with Thorpe-Bowker.

James Bennett Pty Ltd is Australia's leading library supplier and after you have registered with Thorpe-Bowker, they often generate an automatic purchase order for books under $100. This means they search and collect copies of new books arriving in the marketplace all the time. They then assess its compatibility to a library's requests. They put the book and the library together – rather like a dating service! You are eligible to electronically submit title information to **Global Books in Print** as well as the **Australian Books in Print** and the **Bookseller + Publisher** magazine. The Bowker database is also used by booksellers and libraries.

Promotion

When it comes to promotion – it is all about your stamina and self-esteem!

It really does depend on how bold you are as to how much you ask of others in this part of the process. Keep reminding yourself that as long as you are not hurting or taking from anyone, the worst that can happen is that the answer can be "No". Once you understand this, you will be on target for a promotional campaign to help sell those books.

There is a veritable raft of ideas you can use and it is one other area where authors are happy to share their expertise. The important thing is to tailor your promotional strategy to the extent with which you are comfortable. There is no point trying to secure radio interviews or offer to host a book launch or author talk if you are terrified at the thought of speaking in public – unless of course, you are willing to step out of your comfort zone! Have a look at the results from the SWOT analysis exercise again. Remember, this simple tool helps you discover which promotional activities best 'fit' you.

Now for some real action items.

Book Reviews

Previously, I have suggested sending out galley or mock copies of your book for review. This should have taken place before the printing of the book, to secure reviews to include on the cover or inside pages. The review process is invaluable as it lends credence to your book as well as reaffirming to a potential buyer that they are certainly not wasting their money.

Once your book has been published, it is time to send out review copies to literary magazines and book reviewers. Consider the publications which would most likely be viewed by your target market. Then check them out yourself. Find the book reviews, take notes on who has actually written the book review, search for contact addresses and send them your book with a professional cover letter to request their review. Alternatively, write your own in the form of a press release (including a picture of the front cover in the article), and send it out there! You never know – it may be a slow news day or someone may have been a little tardy and not prepared their own reviews.

Book Launch

Oh, the book launch! This creates an opportunity for the community to engage with you as you host a special function to officially launch your book into the stratosphere! Guests inevitably have either a sense of anticipation or a sense or obligation to purchase - this will help you on your way and it is certainly great for your confidence. Remember, publicity is free, but you have to pay for advertising.

For *I Can Do Anything*, I held the launch at a friend's shop, That Kid's Shop, and invited the media. I had two of the baby stars of the book in situ (on rugs looking stunning) and the local WIN TV attended. I had contacted the news desk a couple of weeks out and then again the day before. I chose a morning launch (TV crews are always flat out after 3 pm), and fortunately it was a lovely slow story day! Another girlfriend captured the entire event on camera, and I used the photos in a press release which I sent to the local newspaper that afternoon. It appeared in the weekend edition.

As it comes time for you to organise your own book launch, keep the following points in mind:

- Decide on a date and make sure your book will be printed by then.
- Book a suitable venue, it really can be anywhere – just make sure it is accessible.
- Contact the guests by telephone then follow up with hand written invitations.
- Invite a well-known individual to officially launch your book for you – it makes more sense to ask someone you know but, failing that, contacting your person of choice will be like everything else we have covered – do your research, be professional and be prepared. The worst thing they can say is "no", so do it!
- Contact the media and invite them as guests, and tell them who else is coming.
- Send media a press release. Think of a 'hook' to make them read it, tell them about the book and its evolution and don't forget all your contact details.
- Organise an official photographer for the event, to be sure that there are photos available for promotional purposes, whether or not the media accept your invitations.
- Plan unique activities to entice children and their parents to attend – activities, crafts, competitions, readings and anything else which would create a good morning, afternoon or evening out for a family.
- Get the word out about your book launch – through local newspapers, industry newsletters, local libraries and so on.
- Organise the catering. Self-cater or outsource to very, very good friends or to a catering business. All expenses are tax deductible, after all.
- Organise refreshments. Remember to be appropriate – it is difficult to stomach wine for breakfast!

- Have a lectern where you will deliver the wittiest, most charming speech ever.
- Have a gimmick, but make it appropriate to your book. You will have worked this out when you work out what is different about your book – food, themes, something unique and interesting to appeal for your target market.
- Decorate according to the theme of your book. Be creative.
- Have a table and a number of good 'signing' pens – you will be busy selling and signing if you have done everything properly!
- Ensure that you have organised payment methods. Will you have EFTPOS capabilities? If not, indicate payment will be by cash or cheque only.

Venue

The venue doesn't necessarily have to be a bookstore or hall. It can be a school, library, gallery, at a literary lunch or conference, a park – or even the zoo, if there are animals involved in the story.

> Aleesah Darlison organised a Puggle's Picnic, to support the promotion of her book, **Puggle's Problem**. It was a joint venture with the Featherdale Wildlife Park, and included games, activities, crafts, and a live echidna feeding. It was a fun day out for the whole family.

Activities

The activities to be planned are very important. They need to link to the theme of the book, and give an incentive for people to attend. Gone are the days of launching a book with a simple speech and the opportunity to purchase. If you want to draw a crowd, plan some unique activities and then get the word about, so people will get excited about the event.

> At Deb Pacholke's launch of **Eric The Echidna**, held at the Toowoomba Regional Library, she entertained children and their parents with a reading and invited children to colour in echidna masks they could then take home.

Plan to involve the audience. Rather than them just standing there and listening, be sure to organise activities that will enable them to get excited and become involved, such as competitions and activities or crafts. Remember that you are appealing to a target audience of children (the readership age that your book is written for) and their parents.

> Angela Sunde's first book **Pond Magic** had a French theme to it. She heavily promoted a launch for her book full of family fun and it had two particularly interesting competitions. The first was a prize for the best French costume, with children and their parents invited to participate. The other was, believe it or not, a burping competition!

Decorations

Go beyond balloons and streamers. Decorate the event in a way that will highlight the themes of the book. Of course, you can include a display with copies of your book and framed original illustrations from the book. But go beyond that, too. If your book is about a little princess, decorate royally with golds and rich colours, and crowns. If it is a book about puppies on a farm, you might even bring in some hay bales and farm tools to create a scene.

Props

Props take decorations a step further. These are items that will actually be used to aid in the presentation, discussion or question-and-answer time. They might include framed photos of items, people or places relevant to the story, video footage on a large TV screen, pieces of equipment, or even animals! In the examples above, a prop for a book about a little princess could be a crown and elegant dress, or even someone dressed up as the main character. In the farm book example, you might even bring in the puppies. Ainsley is already looking forward to the launch of her book, **Slow Down, Sarah!** with the perfect prop in mind. She still has the red 50cc motorbike that she grew up riding on her parents' property. Today, her own children ride it!

> Some authors are very creative in their ideas for interesting props. Again, Aleesah Darlison. She likes to use animals as an interesting attention-grabber at her events. She has actually taken a possum with her to a book launch and subsequent author talks.

Media

Press Releases

If you are going to write, why not write about yourself – you can be your own public relations machine! Other than the book reviews, the construction and distribution of press releases can yield results. Find the tagline (the memorable connection between the product and the market – 'a book no girl can be without', 'save the planet one step at a time', or 'boys, bums and brains').

Next, concentrate on finding the right vehicle – for example **Woman's Day**, for the story about a clever mother (who has written and illustrated her own children's picture book focusing on toilet training), or **Brisbane's Child** for the story about a child author.

Next, make sure your timing is right. For example, Byron Bay journalist and cookbook writer Victoria Cosford was interviewed for the magazine **50 Something** just before the Byron Bay Writers' Festival, where she was a guest speaker at the festival. Appropriate topic (check), tagline (check), timing (check).

Articles

Again, be bold and get your name out there. Position yourself as an expert and write articles to share knowledge or anecdotes. If you don't get paid for your contribution, at least ask for your name and the name of your book to be included as a contributor, and a web address so people can find you. Start locally – if you live in an area with a local magazine, offer to contribute. Write about the importance of literacy, write about the relevance of art in a community – anything! Just make sure there is a link between you and your work, for example, 'Emma Mactaggart, local author and illustrator'.

Gifts and Competitions

Gifts – yes, freebies! Offer copies to the local newspaper for use in their children's competition pages. Offer copies as prizes for a colouring competition at the local library, on the same day that you do author readings. Give a copy to any school you visit for their library. Offer copies to use for prizes in school or literary magazines. There are usually tonnes of events happening in every local community relating to your target market, and donations of prizes are always welcome.

School Visits

There is no way a school will knock back a free author visit. Mind you, everyone told me not to offer to visit schools on these 'terms'. I used it as 'work experience' and improved my presentation using a live audience. Ask, by way of 'payment', for some space in their newsletter in return and even better, offer a percentage of pre-visit or post-visit sales to the Parents and Friends Association. Even if a parent doesn't pick up the book for their child at this point, they may remember you and ask at the local bookstore.

Alternatively, if you have books in a store, keep them informed of the schools you are visiting. You can distribute order forms before your presentation, maybe offering an incentive discount for pre-purchasing or even better, the possibility of the child having their book signed by the author after the presentation. This probably increases your chances of sales, rather than sending the children home with order forms for collection at a later date. You can also have a stock of books on hand for sale on the day. Nothing like an impulse purchase if you have impressed the audience.

> I have tried all of these methods – and the most successful or lucrative method is to actually be paid for your author visit. It will yield a substantial amount more than the percentage from book sales. Other than promoting yourself to schools through a pamphlet with your rates and your topics, you can make applications to have an agent do this task for you. Agents, like manuscript appraisers and publishers, have application guidelines which they are very prescriptive about. Lists of agents can be found in the **Writers Marketplace** and of course, you guessed it – Google. I found the agent I work with talking to the teachers at the schools. I asked where they 'sourced' their speakers from, *voilà*, the name 'Speaker Ink'.

Internet

Website

It is time to be interactive! It would be particularly ignorant of me to not allude to the changes taking the conventional traditional publishing industry by storm. You are about to launch your product into a market which considers the validity of eBooks, free content, audio books and iPhone apps as acceptable if not preferable in some instances. I particularly love the quote from the contemporary American author Scott Sigler who, when questioned about sharing his work, stated: *"Piracy is not his enemy, obscurity is"*. This has become my mantra, too.

I outsourced my website design to the same graphic designer who produced my logo. Working very closely with the web designers, I knew that I needed more than the single page 'presence' website available in template form. It was really important to work out before construction began (yes, just like building a house) where I wanted all the components located, indeed, what all the components were. Do you want to facilitate sales (therefore needing e-commerce capabilities)? Do you want to host your own blog? Do you want to offer resources for free or for a fee? The list is endless.

The place to begin is to look at what other authors and illustrators are offering with their websites. Methodically note what you like and what you don't like. Add anything else to your list. And then look for a web designer to put it all together. Look at who designed the websites you like the most. Seek referrals from people you know. When you do find a designer you think might be suitable, be sure to notice whether they seem to truly understand your needs, and whether they follow through on what they say they will do. If they cannot be contacted easily or return your phone calls or emails efficiently, beware. We've all heard horror stories of people who had to wait an age for their web designers to get their sites finished. You don't want your promotional strategy held up because of choosing the wrong designer.

Alternatively, it is possible to get started with a website using one of the many of the free website template services, like Word Press, providing something simple to begin with. Do a Google search to find a selection of them. Some free blog services also enable you to create pages which function as a website, too. However, you will need to set it up yourself, though the process for doing so has been created to assist those without strong technological skills. This may suffice as a website until you find it too limiting for what you want to accomplish. At this time, you can upgrade to a custom-designed website.

Online Newsletters and Listings

There are many organisations out there busting to support you. You can join these groups via a membership and then have access to resources, contacts, information (often in the form of industry magazines or e-newsletters), promotional vehicles and more. You alone can determine what you can or cannot afford.

Here are some examples with costs, at the time of publication:

- State Writers Centres (Queensland is $60 per year)
- CBCA ($49.50)
- Australian Society of Authors ($150 per year)
- Illustrators Australia ($192.50)
- Australian Booksellers Association ($185)
- Pass It On by **jackiehosking@bigpond.com** (70 cents per week)

Social Media

Social media is simply about keeping in touch with those you have already met and meeting those with whom you have common interests. It is about building communities. Don't be intimidated by blogging and social networks, they may seem elusive to the uninitiated, yet all provide step-by-step guidelines to joining in the melee!

According to Fiona Crawford, a freelance writer, editor and blogger, '*A blog should not be confused with an online diary – no-one wants to be privy to an over-share – and needs to be well-written and erudite.*' Whether you choose Facebook, YouTube, Twitter, Readit, MySpace or a new platform which I haven't mentioned, your contributions to the world also need to be well written and definitely frequent.

The wonderful thing about researching the inexhaustible number of ways to promote and sell your work is the treasures you discover along the way. The internet offers a world of possibilities. I just Googled 'eBooks' and quickly found sites offering the best free eBooks offered in countries around the world (**www.e-book.com.au/freebooks**).

Don't get too distracted though. Only let yourself spend a limited amount of time each day researching online. Remember, you are an author, an illustrator and maybe a publisher – you don't have time to add 'internet surfer' to your bio!

Whatever social media you choose to engage in, be sure of two things:

1. Ensure that your time spent on social media is actually connecting you to your potential customers (readers), not just to others who are trying to do the same thing as you and promote their books! If you are only connecting with other authors and illustrators, your time could probably best be spent elsewhere.
2. Ensure that your time spent on social media is actually translating into sales. Otherwise, it really is glorified recreation, and once again, your time could probably best be spent elsewhere.

Develop a Plan

Yes, using what you have discovered in the SWOT analysis, and after considering all of the options available to you, create a marketing plan. It sounds complicated, but actually it is rather simple. You have all the information, now it is a matter of collation and action.

One-Time Tasks

These are tasks requiring specific times and dates to be allocated to them, such as book launches and author visits. These tasks will usually focus on setting up your world as a business or relying on the assistance of external stakeholders, such as meeting with the web designer, having your photo taken, and organising your book launch. Once identified, these tasks should be determined in order of need and if necessary, compliance with a budget.

Ongoing Tasks

Determining how to manage ongoing tasks is basically planning ahead for the promotional activities you aim to implement, and putting them into a calendar or schedule. Some tasks will be fairly constant (such as maintaining a blog) or writing a monthly opinion piece or a newsletter. Combine tasks into a schedule of promotional activities. Then you can refer to this regularly to keep you on track.

Once you have identified your one-time and ongoing tasks, insert them into a simple spreadsheet to create a calendar of promotional activities and events over a given period of time. It's that easy!

Like any good friendship, it is really about how much of your energy you are willing to commit to the relationship. Hopefully, the flip-side will be sales, sales, sales so you will be able to give up your day job.

These are just a few suggestions which may help those sales, and of course there are many more. So read as much as you can get your hands on, talk to as many people as you can find and try and think outside the square.

I have presented only a sample of the marketing strategies and tools available to help you market and promote your children's picture book. If you would like to develop your skills and knowledge base further, I recommend two resources:

> 1. Aleesah Darlison is a published children's author, Aleesah's background is as a corporate marketer, and it is obvious! Go to **www.aleesahdarlison.com** for details of Aleesah's exceptional *Marketing & Promoting Your Book* workshop. She also offers various promotional templates and checklists to make marketing your book much easier.

> 2. Palmer Higgs' **The Self Publisher's Marketing Guide** is an excellent, interactive guide to all the various aspects of marketing from researching your target market to different promotional strategies you can implement. Get your hands on it as soon as you can!

Honestly, the world is your oyster. Now go and get it...

In the Words of a Child

"When I first published my book, I gave my closest family and friends a copy of my book for Christmas presents, and after that there were a number of people who wanted a copy. So I reprinted and sold copies to those people. I am currently working towards placing my book in a local bookshop with order by consignment."

Blake, age 9, author & illustrator **Hamish and His Hovercraft**, about the process of selling his book.

Conclusion

The Last Pep Talk

It is time for you to fly.

Anything in life we consider, any endeavour, any relationship, any challenge, comes with its own positives and negatives – and only you can decide how much of your heart and soul you wish to contribute. Like all of these events, those who may only be as little as one step in front of you will want to share all they know about the process. This is the incredible gift which comes from anyone who is passionate about an endeavour.

We have tried to balance the need to be prescriptive and tell you everything you need to know with the very real need for you to discover much of this yourself. That you have even read this far is a tribute to your stamina and your resolve.

Follow each step – and even step out and do some further research of your own. You might be surprised at what you discover.

Most of all have fun!

Truly, giving the gift of words, whether to thousands or to just a few who gather around you, is a most precious gift. You may as well sprinkle those words with a little laughter.

Enjoy the process – you can do it!

Epilogue

I wish I wish I WISH...

If you have read this far, I can't help but be terribly impressed. Ainsley and I have both loved the process of bringing this book to life and sharing it with you. We hope you are equally entranced by the process which is Child Writes. Whilst this book promises to guide the reader through the process of creating a children's picture book, it predominantly remains, in disguise, a guide for those wishing to teach children how to write and illustrate their own picture books.

I wish, I wish, I WISH for all of the books the children have written so far (and those books you, as the adult may guide other children to write and illustrate), to be made available within mini-libraries for children anywhere who are in crisis. In oncology and hospital wards, in places like Relationships Australia (where the adults supporting children may be in need themselves), in donation boxes at Christmas time via The Smith Family or St Vincent de Paul, and in all Pyjama Foundation libraries, accessible to readers who focus on foster children...

There is something incredibly empowering for a child to see such an accomplished product made by another child. The response we wish for (after the wonderment has faded) from a child who has realised the book in their hands has been written and illustrated by a child their age is this:

"Well, if they can, I can!"

Children writing for children supporting children can work wonders.

Please, contact us if you are curious about joining Child Writes as a printing partner or as a distributor or as a champion or as a Child Writes tutor for the Child Writes program. Anything is possible.

Jetstar has taken Child Writes on board, showing a selection from the Child Writes library in their in-flight entertainment. How exciting to think of the children's words and pictures flying! Jetstar. Thank you.

If you tried to invent a program which embraced literature and supported literacy; which encouraged lateral thinking and the ability to see the whole, as well as understanding the components; which encouraged children to be the creator, the appraiser, the editor, the designer and the presenter; which ensured children contextualised their existence within the broader community – it certainly would be difficult. It has only been by evolution, trial and error that Child Writes has the potential to address all these facets, whilst giving children a voice and ensuring an increase in their self-efficacy. Without you, this would not be possible.

For it is the right of every child to have their voice heard. The more the merrier!

Useful **Resources**

You just can't go another day without looking at the following useful books and addresses:

Essential Websites:

National Library of Australia

www.nla.gov.au

This is an indispensible website for information. Search for the information for publishers. ISBN, Legal Deposit, Cataloguing-in-Publication information – it is all there, with up-to-date links for organisations like the Australian Publishers Association, The Australian Society of Authors and the Australian Writers' Guild.

Bowker-Thorpe

www.thorpe.com.au/support/support_links.htm

Don't even think about waiting another minute before looking at the Thorpe website. Not only is this the key to obtaining your ISBN, the directory is the most comprehensive in Australia (there, that was a bold statement)!

www.thorpe.com.au/forms/files/publish.pdf

It is a distinct pleasure to read something which is so right. This is a guide for self publishers and really, truly, – you must go and download a copy now – it may have saved you reading this book!

Writers' Groups

www.asauthors.org

For links to writers' centres around the country, including regional centres.

Lists of Distributors

www.publishers.asn.au

Australian and overseas distributors

Recommended Websites:

All About Drawings

www.allaboutdrawings.com

The home of Sketchy News – a site with everything you need to know about drawing. The site is written and managed by Kerry, who is approachable, considerate, thoughtful and timely in her reply. Being part of the world of *All About Drawings* is like having a tutor in your studio!

Aleesah Darlison

www.aleesahdarlison.com

Aussie Reviews

www.aussiereviews.com

The home of great reviews of great Australian books and more. Note: if you are an author or publisher hoping to have a book reviewed, please read the review policy before making contact.

The Australian Writers' Marketplace

www.awmonline.com.au

Every contact you need to succeed in the writing business.

Buzzwords

www.buzzwordsmagazine.com

The latest buzz on books for children.

Pass it On

www.jackiehoskingpio.wordpress.com

PASS IT ON is a weekly, online, interactive, networking newsletter for those involved with or interested in the children's writing and illustration industry.

Fear is Power

www.fearispower.com.au

Self Efficacy – my favourite term for the year. I heard psychologist Anthony Gunn discussing his book **Raising Happy Confident Children** on the radio (I know – not via Facebook/YouTube or Twitter). The best thing is his work offers sensible, timely, achievable ways to problemsolve whatever crisis is at hand. Sometimes, if you are multi tasking as a parent and a writer (which, whilst both require incredible energy, are polarised. One is a very giving enterprise and the other takes), well… you may need a little help.

Frane Lessac

www.franelessac.com

Frane Lessac is a prolific illustrator based in Perth. I met her in Toowoomba and was delighted at how supportive she was of the Child Writes program and how enthusiastically generous she was with advice for me.

Illustrators Australia

www.illustratorsaustralia.com

This site offers folios from again, an extraordinary range of illustrators.

Science Fiction and Fantasy Writers of America

www.sfwa.org/for-authors/writers-beware/thumbs-down-agency

Writers Beware – a publishing industry watchdog group sponsored by the Science Fiction and Fantasy Writers of America – lists 'publishing' companies who are vanity publishers in disguise! The site focuses on businesses using 'abusive' practices such as fee-charging and paid-editing. The list is continually updated, so keep returning to the site.

Mark Svendsen

www.marksvendsen.com

Mark Svendsen is a gentleman who just happens to be particularly well educated, writes industriously and obviously has amazing time management skills when you see his workload! I also met Mark here in Toowoomba – at a dinner party! His comments about the writing industry being supportive, thoughtful and generous with the sharing of knowledge and advice rang true. He introduced me to Helen Bain at Speakers Ink. I include him here as a true example of how the industry works!

Palmer Higgs

www.palmerhiggs.com.au

If you have decided to self publish your book, you have a couple of options for producing it. You can do everything yourself or you can so some of it or you can ask someone else to do it for you. If you need help with any or all components of your book production journey, regardless of how you approach it from a publishing model standpoint – get in touch with Palmer Higgs. They offer a generous amount of information via their website, all of which is indispensible. They also have an uncanny knack of interpreting what services you may or may not need, without you having to articulate it yourself. This is a brilliant 'must have' attribute which should be one of the key determinants for choosing who will partner you on your journey!

The Style File

www.thestylefile.com (Rebecca Berrett)

This particularly interesting website offers examples of work from an extraordinary range of illustrators. Rebecca is one illustrator featured. She is a tutor in another life when she can be dragged from her studio and is responsible for a very large number of passionate graduates from the Macgregor Summer School at USQ, Toowoomba, where she teaches how to illustrate children's books. I graduated from her class in 2006, and have loved the journey ever since.

Space Jock

www.spacejock.com.au

I Googled 'print-on-demand publishing' and Simon's site was at the top of the pile. He had an interesting description of POD and I then noticed his list of articles. He, has a publisher, has attempted self publishing, gives away an eBook, has sample chapters, has an agent, has a great website, blogs madly, and shares his professional experiences in conversant articles. He, has advertisers on the site (so generates an alternate income), has a Google subscription link (now I know why he was at the top of the list!), is a community member and therefore contributor of LibraryThing and Linkedin and of course, Twitter – AND he has 1952 friends on Myspace, so has the social networking thing happening – he uses multiple platforms for his work, (book, eBook, games). He really does everything everyone tells you to do!

The only piece of information I couldn't find was an indication of when his website was last updated, but I am sure that says more about my research techniques than Simon's site.

Now all I have to do is actually read one of his books!

Writers' Web

www.writersweb.com.au
This fabulous new model of publishing is available to you – as a writer, a reader, a reviewer or as a publisher.

BlogSpot

erictheechidna.blogspot.com
Read about how Deb Pacholke offers her self published book via her BlogSpot.

Recommended Books:

Australian Book Contracts

Compiled by the Australian Society of Authors
Print Contracts / Digital Contracts
Keesing Press
ISBN 0 9587072 1 9

You do know you may need this. Remember, start how you mean to finish. Of course you need to know all about contracts. And here is the guide that will simplify it for you.

Editing Made Easy

Written by Bruce Kaplan
ISBN 978 01430017 1 3

A friendly, practical guide for writers and editors and anyone who wants to write well. It is absolutely fantastic! It's simple, short, clear and makes the editing process easy, as it says...

Inside Book Publishing

Written by Giles Clark and Angus Phillips
Taylor and Francis e-library, 2008
ISBN 978-0-203-34154-4

Clark and Phillips have produced a definitive guide of the history of publishing. I was fascinated by the insights into the necessary cannibalisation of publishing houses in the search for the most productive lists, especially as the costs of the traditional industry continue to increase.

Painless Grammar

Written by Rebecca Elliott Ph.D.
Barron's Educational Series; 2 edition (August 1, 2006)
ISBN 978-0764134364

Love it – though that may not be grammatically correct! Elliott's method of guiding through the rules and intricacies of grammar ensures the process is indeed painless. It is one of those little books which should remain on your desk and which you will refer to so often, it will not gather dust.

Print-on-Demand Book Publishing

Written by the insightful and progressive Morris Rosenthal
Published by Foner Books
ISBN 0-9723801-3-2

What is refreshing is Rosenthal's understanding of the industry, yet he is not beholden to any conventions. It is rather like looking outside the square as he comfortably analyses the pros and cons of the conventions of publishing and what the future holds. It is refreshing and liberating to read this, as there is a future for the book!

Self Publishing Made Simple

Written by Euan Mitchell
Overdog Press
ISBN: 9780975797907

This is a definitive, clear and practical guide for the Australian self publishing industry. It is extremely practical, and goes through the stages of preparation, pre-press, printing, distribution and marketing.

The Australian Writers' Marketplace

Compiled and Edited by the Queensland Writers Centre,
Originally by Rhonda Whitton in 1997
ISBN 978-1-920892-35-7

In Australia, this is known as the 'bible' in the industry. Produced biennially, it is a detailed and up-to-date reference book with all the contacts you will need, plus a healthy sprinkling of anecdotes from publishers, writers and more. You can also subscribe to the online version.

The New Drawing on the Right Side of the Brain

Written by the inimitable Betty Edwards, 1979, 1999
Published by Jeremy P. Tacher/Putnam
ISBN 0-87477-424-1

For those of you who believe they can't draw — purchasing and devouring this book page by page is a must. Not only is it exhilarating spending time immersed in the writing of a professional of such long standing, it is Edwards' passionate belief that everyone can draw, which leaves an impression. Indeed, everyone can draw — you just need to learn how.

www.drawright.com about the magic which is Betty Edwards' work!

The Self publisher's Marketing Guide

Written by Debbie Higgs
Palmer-Higgs Publishing
ISBN: 978-0-9807867-7-4

This is an interactive and extremely helpful guide for self publishers to research, plan and implement their own relatively inexpensive marketing campaign. It is well worth the investment, and it takes a subject which may previously seem very complex, and makes it extremely simple to both understand and do.

The Seven Basic Plots

Researched and written over thirty years by the indefatigable Christopher Booker, 2004.
Published by Continuum Books
ISBN 0-8264-5209-4

A 'must-purchase' tome from an incredibly passionate author. Booker has demonstrated the findings of his research on the stories you are most likely to know. What is equally fascinating is the introduction to many stories which you do not know, yet will be familiar with as he describes the different models for basic plots. It is really fascinating reading.

Writing Down the Bones – Freeing the Writer Within

Written by the peaceful, intuitive Natalie Goldberg, 1986, 2005
Published by Shambhala
ISBN 978-0-8773-375-1

From the guru of writing, Goldberg intuitively and intelligently weaves her two passions of writing and yoga. Being in the right state of mind to be creative is essential to writing. This is an echo of Edward's book about drawing. If you are determined to write and illustrate your own children's picture book – you need both of these in your life.

Writing Picture Books

Written by Ann Whitford
ISBN: 9781582975566

This is a comprehensive book on writing style and structure for picture books, and is an invaluable reference for evaluating your work and providing rewriting options which can turn a lacklustre story into a masterpiece! An extremely useful resource.

Writers Centres and Online Listings

The Northern Rivers Writers' Centre

info@nrwc.org.au
www.nrwc.org.au
As splendid hosts of the Byron Bay Writers Festival, the Northern Rivers Writers Centre keeps you up-to-date with what is happening via an eBulletin and a monthly magazine. The festival is like a lovely massage for your mind – at the time, it is exhilarating and invigorating while you are there, and afterwards, you feel a very warm glow as the months lead you away from the weekend!

The Queensland Writers Centre

www.qwc.asn.au

The ACT Writers Centre

www.actwriters.org.au

Northern Territory Centre – Ozwrite

www.ntwriters.com.au

NSW Writers' Centre

www.nswrwriterscentre.org.au

Victorian Writers' Centre

www.vwc.org..au

South Australian Writers' Centre

www.sawc.org..au

Sydney Writers' Centre

www.sydneywriterscentre.com.au

Fellowship of Australian Writers Western Australia

www.fawwa.org.au

Glossary

A Book

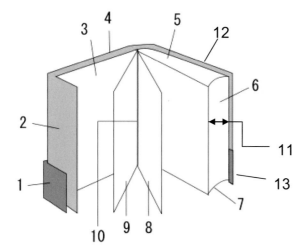

1	Belly band
2	Flap
3	Endpaper
4	Book cover
5	Top edge
6	Fore edge
7	Tail edge
8	Right page
9	Left page
10	Gutter
11	Guts (all the pages)
12	Short edge
13	Long edge

A book can be described as having a:

- Spread – when the book is open and you can see the left page and the right page together
- Gutter – the centre of the book when it is open at a spread. Depending on the binding and how the reader holds the book, it is vital no important information (either text or picture) is in the gutter as you may not see it!
- Leaf – is a page.
- Section – is a number of pages, divisible by four. A children's picture book is two sections, sixteen pages each, hence thirty-two pages. Relates originally to the binding process when the books were sewn together and how the pages were printed.

Parts Of A Book

Imprint Page - (Chapter 6 Plan it and 10 Build it) – this is often a dedicated page, which contains all the following information:

- **Dedication** – no doubt you are interested in acknowledging those around you without whom the project would not be possible. It is the most stunning way you can say 'thank you.'

- **ISBN** – it is yours and yours alone! As soon as you are on the path to completion – apply for the ISBN so you have heaps of time to receive the information back before going to the printer. No need to request the ISBN fast tracking, which costs more money.

The International Standard Book Number (ISBN) is a 13-digit number that uniquely identifies books and book-like products published internationally. While an ISBN is not mandatory, and does not provide copyright on a work, it is the principal worldwide ordering device for the international book trade and library market. **www.nla.gov.au**

ISBNs are used to specifically identify a title with a particular format, edition and content; usually for information accession (libraries) or for ordering purposes (libraries and bookshops). **www.thorpe.com.au**

- **Cataloguing-in-Publication Data** – helps people find you. Once you have the ISBN, apply for *CiP* immediately – not as the book is going to the printer!
  Cataloguing-in-Publication (CiP) is a free service offered to publishers by the National Library of Australia to provide a catalogue record for publications which have not yet been published. **www.nla.gov.au**

- **About the book** – include information which may be of use for those who are passionate about books and yearn for a little more information or those who study books: the font description, the medium used to produce the illustrations, style notes of any type. Be generous with the information.

- **Publisher** – you would be mad if you didn't include contact information – you never know who is reading the book and who may be interested in procuring the rights to making it into a movie! (Okay, that was a stretch, but seriously, include contact information!)

- **Other books** – consumers are interesting creatures! Chances are if they like the book in their hands, they will look for books belonging to the same author / illustrator in the future, or look to purchase ones written in the past. Think of this book a bit like a brochure!

Blurb

On the back of most books, you will find an eloquently succinct description about the book. There may be reviews included, or other notations appropriate to that book (like the author is WAY famous and because you saw him and LOVED him on the telly, well, you will love his book!) Anyway, if your book is a work of fiction, you must promise the book is a 'good read'. You have to be able to convince the reader there is something in the book for them and they will be happy. Use emotive words, keep it brief and don't give away the ending!

Blurt

On the inside back cover this is what we call a micro – curriculum vitae. Given most of my authors are under the age of 12, their CV is not very extensive – but is it useful to the reader to identify with the author / illustrator if possible. A biography often lends a degree of legitimacy, ensuring the reader that the author is indeed in a position to write a book which you will like!

Galley

A galley is a bound 'proof' which can be used for promotional purposes or to seek the input of other readers pre-print. (You know how books have those comments by other people or reviews – well, they get to see a galley, are asked to reply with a thought, and this is then included in the final print.) Usually they are pretty cheaply produced, often paper back or handbound.

Illustrator

If I said 'you' – it well could be. For me, whilst I love drawing, I find I don't give the discipline enough time (hence only two finished books – and ten in waiting!). Illustrators can produce a finished product which differs from that of an artist. For example, a watercolour may look divine in a frame, but when it is copied, the colour can be non-existent! The key is the reproducibility of the image.

Manuscript

A manuscript is a manual creation, which means 'written by hand'. This is why publishers insist you don't send them the 'original manuscript'. Its definition has broadened now as it is understood a manuscript can include writing, which may be set down via a typewriter or a printer, then submitted to a publisher or a printer in preparation for publication.

Unsolicited manuscript – you haven't been asked to send your work to the publisher have you? If you have done so, it is considered an unsolicited manuscript.

Solicited manuscript – wow – they want your stuff – get moving!

Publisher

This is a person within a business whose priority is to facilitate the process of production and distribution of literature. They assess the viability of a manuscript to translate to sales which will exceed the costs of production. This includes its literary merit, the marketability of the product and the author as well as the ability for the author to contribute at all stages in the process.

Writer

YOU! Look in the mirror – say to yourself, "I am a writer". Make sure you include it on every piece of documentation which requires 'occupation' to be stated, you say it when people ask you what you do you are a writer!

Self Publisher

The author becomes the publisher and is responsible for all tasks associated with the production, distribution and promotion of a book. Subsequently, the author becomes the risk taker.

Subsidy Publisher

They offer the author a cooperative agreement, taking on some of the tasks (usually strongly focusing on the distribution and promotion of the book), sharing the associated costs at the beginning of the project, promising a return once sales have surpassed a predetermined level.

Vanity Publisher

This is a printer offering all the services required for book production for a fee. The client is the author, not the book buyer, even though the promise will be made for promotion.

Illustration Stuff

Bleed

This is when the illustration is constructed without a border, meaning the printer can take it off the page and once it is trimmed, there will still be no white surrounds. This is only really relevant if you want to be able to tell if something is printed on a local photocopier and bound (it will have a white border) or whether something has gone through a more rigorous printing set-up.

Render

To render means adding the colour to the illustration. One style of illustration is to prepare the image, maybe using an illustrator pen (which is waterproof and fadeproof) to outline or make marks which are visible through the colour medium. The children use pen then watercolour.

De-stick

This is referring to masking tape or any other adhesive tape. Place it onto your jeans or the carpet, press down and remove. The tackiness will be reduced but it will not be rendered useless! Use 'de-sticked' tape to put your illustrations on the wall, so you can take a few steps backwards and have another look from another perspective.

Monochromatic

The use of one colour with various shades or tonal layers is generally called monochromatic.

Business Stuff

Copyright

This exists as soon as pen is put to paper and it lasts for seventy years after the author is d.e.d! The phrase 'All Rights Reserved' means you can't do anything without permission.

Creative Commons

www.creativecommons.org.au
You can release your story under licence, which allows readers to copy, communicate, distribute and perform and adapt work, even commercially. More often than not, it is simply the request of the original author that you acknowledge them.

Legal Deposit

This is when you donate a copy of your book to the National Library of Australia and your state library. (You should send a copy to your local library as well.)

Legal Deposit is a requirement under the Copyright Act 1968 for publishers and self publishing authors to deposit a copy of any work published in Australia with the National Library and the deposit libraries in your home state. Legal Deposit ensures that Australian publications are preserved for use now and in the future. **www.nla.gov.au**

Public Domain

Public domain is designation given to content that is no longer subject to copyright protection. It is therefore available for anyone to use freely for whatever purpose.

Terms of Trade

These are all the things you need to consider regarding selling your book. Not only do you have to determine the recommended retail price, you also have to consider - Are you going to offer discounts, how long can the bookseller take before paying your invoice, is there a cost delivering your books into store or do you charge freight, is there a cost for small orders, can they send books back and what to do when your book is faulty.

USB Flash Drive

Is a data storage device which has a USB interface. A universal bus is a specification to establish communication between two devices. The flash drive is fondly known here as 'the stick'.

150

Permissions

From Kerry at **www.allaboutdrawings.com**

"It was lovely to receive your email, thank you. You are very welcome to use whatever you like from my site. I would be honoured to help you, my site is designed to encourage everyone to draw so it's wonderful to get the word around in any way possible."

From Louise Schultze CEO **www.iBidAM.com**

"Thanks for your email message. What a great idea. I love it. I wrote a series of short stories from the age of 14-17 that was semi-published (only because an already published author got hold of them and convinced her publisher to give me a go). So I only made it into libraries and schools. But the idea that a book was written by a teenager for teenagers was what they liked the most. And as an avid writer who uses words to empower children in my home, I know you are definitely onto something special. And with that, it would be an honour if you wanted to quote me."

From Anthony Gunn, Psychologist **www.fearispower.com.au**

"Thank you for your kind words about my interview on Life Matters (ABC) and for sending me a copy of your book. The work you're doing looks fascinating and very unique. If my quotes are of use then feel free to use them. I wish you all the best with your work. Kind regards."

152

Bibliography

In order of their appearance in the text

CHAPTER 1 – Imagine it

Gunn, Anthony; **Raising Confident, Happy Children**, Hardie Grant Books, 2010
ISBN 978 17406 6749 4

Edwards, Dr Betty; **Drawing on the Right Side of the Brain**, Tacher, 1999
ISBN 978 08747 7424 5

Shelley, Mary; **Frankenstein**, Bantam Classic, 1984
ISBN 978 05532 1247 1

Moloney, James; **A Bridge to Wiseman's Cove**, UQP, 2001
ISBN 978 07022 3322 7

Sendak, Maurice; **Where the Wild Things Are**, Harpers Collins, 1963
ISBN 978 00644 3178 1

Wild, Margaret; **Jenny Angel**, Penguin Aus. 2002
ISBN 978 01405 425 8

Mastnak, Rosemary; **Dancing With Grandma**, Hardie Grant Egmont, 2008
ISBN 978 19212 8890 6

Booker, Christopher; **The Seven Basic Plot, Why We Tell Stories**, Continuum, 2006
ISBN 978 08264 8037 8

Szabo, Domonkos; **The Wet Season March**, Boogie Books (ebook) April 2011
ISBN 978 1 921926 46 4

CHAPTER 2 – Write it

Goldberg, Natalie; **Writing Down the Bones**, Shambhala, 2010
978 15903 0794 6, expanded edition

Jane, Zacharey; **The Life Boat**, UQP, 2011
ISBN 978 07022 3642 6

Jane, Zacharey; **Tobias Blow**, UQP, 2011
ISBN 978 07022 3876 5

Sparrow, Rebecca; **The Girl Most Likely**, UQP, 2003
ISBN 978 07022 3345 6

Sparrow, Rebecca; **The Day Nick McGowan Came to Town**, UQP, 2006
ISBN 978 7022 3551 1

Legge, David; **Bamboozled**, Scholastic Australia, 1995
ISBN 978 05904 7989 9

Lukeman, Noah; **The First Five Pages**, Simon & Schuster, 1999
ISBN 978 06848 5743 5

English, Abbey; **Maltie**, Boogie Books (ebook) April 2011
ISBN 978 19219 2645 7

CHAPTER 3: Evaluate it

Suess, Dr; **Green Eggs and Ham**, Random House Books for Young Readers, 1st Ed, 1960
ISBN 978 05833 2420 5

Suess, Dr; **Hop on Pop,** Beginner Books, 1st Ed, 1963
ISBN 978 03948 0029 5

Rowan, Nicholas; **James**, Boogie Books (ebook) April 2011
ISBN 978 19219 2648 8

CHAPTER 4: Edit it

Kalplan, Bruce; **Editing Made Easy**, Penguin, 2001
ISBN 978 06463 6907 5

Neucom, Madelaine; **The Gumnut Blossom Challenge**, Boogie Books (ebook) April 2011
ISBN 978 19219 2666 2

Neucom, Madelaine; **Gloomy Gus Turns Around**, Boogie Books (ebook) April 2011
ISBN 978 19219 2683 9

CHAPTER 5: Proofread it

Haeusler, Nicole; **Glendora**, Boogie Books (eBook) April 2011
ISBN 978 19219 2695 2

Haeusler, Nicole; **Mateship for Sure**, Boogie Books (ebook) April 2011
ISBN 978 19219 2656 3

Haeusler, Nicole; **Best Buds**, Boogie Books (Middle Ridge Writers Group 2007)
ISBN 978 09803 0081 9

CHAPTER 6: Appraise it

Mactaggart, Emma; **Lily, Fabourama, Glamourama**, Boogie Books, 2004
ISBN-10: 19208 55238

Fitton, Isabel; **No Problem**, Boogie Books (ebook) April 2011
ISBN 978 19219 2679 2

CHAPTER 7: Plan it

Oliver, Narelle; **The Very Blue Thingamajig**, Scholastic, 2004
ISBN 978 18629 1527 5

Carle, Eric; **The Very Hungry Caterpillar**, Philomel, 1981
ISBN 978 03992 0853 9

Mactaggart, Emma; **I Can Do Anything**, TEC, 2003
ISBN-10 192085238

Rogers, Lissy; **'Zz' is for Zebra**, Boogie Books (ebook) April 2011
ISBN 978 19219 2670 9

CHAPTER 8: See it

Spudvilas, Anne; **The Pheasant Prince**, Penguin, 2007
ISBN 978 06700 7054 1

Brown, Ashlee; **I Want A Friend**, Boogie Books (Middle Ridge Writers Group 2008)
ISBN 978 09803 0082 6

CHAPTER 9: Feel it

Lessac, Franee; **Ned Kelly and the Green Sash**, Walter Books Australia, 2010
ISBN 978 19211 5087 6

Base, Graeme; **The Waterhole**, Harry N. Abrams, 2001
ISBN 978 08109 4568 5

Mactaggart, Sarah & House, Emma; **BFF Best Friends Forever**, Boogie Books (eBook) April 2011
ISBN 978 19219 2669 3

CHAPTER 10: Draw it

Edwards, Dr Betty; **Drawing on the Right Side of the Brain**, Tacher, 1999, 2nd revised and enlarged ed.
ISBN 978 08747 7424 5

Early, Margaret; **Sleeping Beauty**, Harry N. Abrams, 1993
ISBN 978 08109 3835 9

Early, Margaret; **William Tell**, Harry N. Abrams, 1991
ISBN 978 08109 3854 0

Perrottet, Fred; **Making Friends**, Boogie Books (ebook) April 2011
ISBN 978 19219 2687 7

CHAPTER 11: Illustrate it

Carnavas, Peter; **Jessica's Box**, New Frontier, 2008
ISBN 978 1921 04291 1

Base, Graeme; **The Waterhole**, Harry N. Abrams, 2001
ISBN 978 08109 4568 5

Alber, Josef; **Interaction of Colour**, Yale University Press
ISBN 978 03001 1595 6

Robertston-Cuninghame, Tanya; **Colour Booklet**, Boogie Books, 2011
ISBN 978 19218 7198 6

Edwards, Dr Betty; **Drawing on the Right Side of the Brain**, Tacher, 1999
ISBN 978 08747 7424 5

Sendak, Maurice; **Where the Wild Things Are**, Harpers Collins, 1963
ISBN 978 00644 3178 1

Carle, Eric; **The Very Hungry Caterpillar**, Philomel, 1981
ISBN 978 03992 0853 9

Grigg, Lachlan; **The Dognapping**, Boogie Books (ebook) April 2011
ISBN 978 19219 2657 0

CHAPTER 12: Share it

Dale, Stephanie; **My Pilgrim's Heart**, Voyager Moon, 2011
ISBN 978 17429 8055 3

Dale, Stephanie; **Hymn for the Wounded Man**, Voyager Moon, 2010
ISBN 978 09807 0431 0

The Australian Writers Marketplace, Queensland Writers Centre, 2011/2012
ISBN 978 19214 8815 3

Ardonetto, Alexandra; **The Shadow Thief**, Harper Collins 2007
ISBN 978 07322 8618 7

O'Dowd, Annie; **Sea Gem and the Land of Ice**, Pan Macmillan Australia, 2006
ISBN 978 14050 3754 9

O'Dowd, Annie; **Left Shoe and the Foundling**, Pan Macmillan Australia, 2005
ISBN 978 14050 3688 7

O'Dowd, Annie; **Marigold and the Dark**, Pan Macmillan Australia, 2005
ISBN 978 1405 0368 9

O'Dowd, Annie; **Tumblegrass and the Bushfire**, Pan Macmillan Australia, 2008
ISBN 978 03304 2388 5

Bernard, Andre; **Rotten Rejections**, Pushcart Press, 1990
ISBN 978 18888 8904 8

Pacholke, Deb; **Eric the Echidna**, Harbed Inc, 2009
ISBN 978 06465 1309 6

Birminham, John; **He Died With a Felafel in His Hand**, Duffy & Snellgrove, 1994
ISBN 978 18759 8921 8

Blakeney, Yvonne; **Where's Elf**, Self published, 2009
ISBN 978 09806 5190 4

Bruggemann, Emily; **Too Busy Lizzie**, Boogie Books (ebook) April 2011
ISBN 978 19219 2640 2

Bruggemann, Emily; **Lizzie in the Bush**, Boogie Books (Sacred Heart Writers' Group 2009)
ISBN 978 09803 0082 6

CHAPTER 13: Build it

Mactaggart, Emma; **I Can Do Anything**, TEC, 2003
ISBN-10 192085238

Base, Graeme; **The Waterhole**, Harry N. Abrams, 2001
ISBN 978 08109 4568 5

Mactaggart, Emma; **Lily, Fabourama**, Glamourama, Boogie Books, 2004
ISBN-10: 19208 55238

Tao, Yonghui; **The Cow That Jumped Over the Moon**, Boogie Books (Middle Ridge Writers Group 2009)
ISBN 978 09803 0084 0

CHAPTER 14: Print it

Carnavas, Peter; **Jessica's Box**, New Frontier, 2008
ISBN 978 1921 04291 1

Mactaggart, Annabel; **The Tea Party Terror**, Boogie Books (ebook) April 2011
ISBN 978 19219 2654 9

CHAPTER 15: Market it

Darlinson, Aleesah; **Puggle's Problem**, Wombat Books, 2010
ISBN 978 19216 3307 2

Pacholke, Deb; **Eric the Echidna**, Harbed Inc, 2009
ISBN 978 06465 1309 6

Sunde, Angela, **Pond Magic**, Penguin, 2010
ISBN 978 01433 0554 5

Hohenhaus, Blake; **Hamish and His Hovercraft**, Boogie Books (ebook) April 2011
ISBN 978 19219 2661 7

Acknowledgements

I have been incredibly fortunate and each day, I seem to meet another person who is excited about Child Writes and wants to help push it along in any way possible, so that more and more children experience the process.

I start with Jan Watkins and Jill Temple, who honestly believed in me. The gaggle who were the Toowoomba Working Party for NAPCAN, Shana, Tarn, Mary-Kate and Ayesha – we just needed to believe giving children a voice made our community a better place. To all Middle Ridge State School, Sacred Heart Primary School and Toowoomba Preparatory School – thank you for allowing me into the classroom. All those at Eidsvold State School – how brave were you testing the first 'by remote' Child Writes program - thank you Rigo and Michelle. The mob at USQ printing services have provided immeasurable support and encouragement which I couldn't do without. Nor the amazing amount of energy and encouragement and wordsmithing from Cherie.

And if only I had an image which said thank you to Michelle, I would use it because words are not enough!

And to *Alex, Tara, Isaac, Jason, Morgan, Sean, Emily, Michael, Carlie, Brianna, Chris, Ingrid, Brooke, Kyle, Adam, Christopher, Grace, Casey, Brooke, Harmony, Tim, Natasha, Elissa, Kayla, Brittany, Katelyn, Callum, Connor, Brooke, Ebony, Lauren, Jake, Beau, Jay, Tahlia, Demier, Erin, Gabby, Adyn, Amy, Anais, Toby, Lewis, Rory, Nicole, Jamie, Haylee, Nicole, Bethany, Lucy, Natasha, Lachlan, Talis, Leticia, Nicole, Tamika, Nell, Candace, Jacob, Victoria, Rebecca, Ashlee, Callan, Breanna, Jessica, Shanae, Emily, Callum, Samantha, Josie, Justin, Kelsee, Isabella, Chantelle, Caitlin, Morgan, Keelie, Maddison, Bella, Abbey, Jessie, Robert, Keely, Lynden, Domonkos, Annie-Lou, Yonghui, Madelaine, Nicholas, Cassidy, Bianca, Paige, Nicole, Blake, Madison, Keelie, Lucy, Ben, Brianna, Sian, Amy, Amber, Will, Hayden, Hollie, Caitlin, Natalie, Kara, Keelee, Amber, Annabel, Bhumika, Callan, Emma, Sarah, Felicity, Flynn, Fred, Hugh, Isabel, Isabel, Lachlan, Laurel, Lorraine, Nicholas, Phoebe, Sara Jane, Shay, Timothy, Rosie, Amber, Gisele, William, Jessica, Carrington, Maddison, Rawdon, Emma, Sarah, Jasmine, Hannah, Phoebe, Emily, Rhiannon, Joshua, Brittany, Sophie, Abbey, Abbey, Brittnee, Isabella, Logan, Lydia, Melanie, Ingrid, Cassidy, Amelia, Bethany, Hayley, Samuel, Mia, Cain, Nikayah, Cody, Dannielle, Malachi, Ktarla-Lee, Shakira, Jazzmin, Tate, Daniel, Cassidy, Nicole, Jayden, Brooke, Zane, Ieshia, Jackson, Zali, Jamie, Tyra, Clinton, Jamal, Larrakia, Jarmbe, Darren, Jared, Skye, Hugh, Brady, Justin, Julian, Claudia, Rodney, Tyler, Aaliyah* – CW graduates from 2005 to 2011 – there is no Child Writes without you.

Ainsley – there is not this book without you – may we continue to give children a voice!

To team Mactaggart – I function because of you.

Emma x

Get on Board With
Child Writes...
Today!

child **writes**™

Whoever you are and whatever you do, if the concept of **Child Writes** has piqued your interest, you are not alone. The unique and multi-faceted nature of this program has gained it enthusiastic support wherever it has been presented. Consider playing a vital role in empowering children, by getting on board with **Child Writes**... today!

NEWSLETTER SIGN UP

Join the Child Writes Community
Sign up for the

Write Now *Newsletter*

'Write Now' is the newsletter for the **Child Writes** program. It is full of exciting **Child Writes** news and developments, announcements on new program locations, book releases by child authors, reviews by child readers, competition details and helpful writing tips. If you would like to be involved in the **Child Writes** story, register to be added to our mailing list, and you will receive the latest copy of the newsletter, each month.

Sign up at:
www.childwrites.com.au

Find Out More

You don't have to be an adult to become a **published** author!

Are you a student who longs to see your words and pictures in print? Perhaps you are the parent of a budding author and illustrator, or you simply know that your child could do with further support in the area of literacy.

All **Child Writes** program participants are eligible to have their books published by Boogie Books (see www.boogiebooks.com.au). Find out about the closest **Child Writes** program in your area, or register your interest to see a program established in your area.

Alternatively, the correspondence version of the program allows students to participate from anywhere, at any time!

> "…the sheer feeling of success of writing, illustrating and publishing a children's book of your own, words cannot describe the feeling. So for anyone out there wanting to publish a book of their own, I encourage you, although it has its up and downs, the feelings are unexplainable."
> **Ashlee, age 12, author & illustrator, 'I Want a Friend'.**

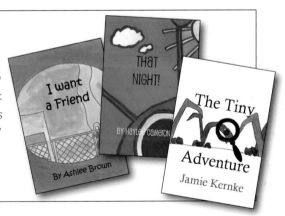

Submit your request for further information at:
www.childwrites.com.au
Select 'Student Participation in the Child Writes program'

You can be **paid** to do what you l♥ve!

Are you a child literacy advocate - a teacher, writer, parent, grandparent, librarian or someone who is simply passionate about children's literacy? **Child Writes** is looking for passionate advocates to become trained tutors of the **Child Writes** program, and extend the reach of **Child Writes** across Australia. Do what you love, make a difference, and generate a part time income at the same time!

Children writing for children, supporting children...

It is a simple ideology which actually works! **Child Writes** is a stunning project, nurturing literacy and creativity, giving children a voice by offering primary school aged children the opportunity to write and illustrate their own children's picture books. These books are published by boutique publisher Boogie Books, complete with ISBNs and an official book launch!

Copies are donated to places (such as hospitals) where children are in crisis... an empowering process for both the child authors and the children who are encouraged by the achievement and generosity of their peers. Every child has their book available for purchase and for the child authors of the most outstanding books, **Child Writes** makes commercial opportunities possible.

The dream is to see the **Child Writes** program available to every child in Australia… but we need YOU, to make that dream a reality!

Submit your request for further information at:

www.childwrites.com.au

Select 'Becoming a tutor of the Child Writes program'

You can make a **difference** to the children in your school!

If you are a teacher, curriculum co-ordinator or Principal, you may be starting to envisage how the **Child Writes** program can positively impact your students and school. Contact **Child Writes** to discuss the various options for running the **Child Writes** program as part of your school curriculum, or as an extra-curricular activity promoted by your school.

See your students excited by literacy and empowered by achievement!

Benefits to your students...

"Why **Child Writes**?" is a question that has many different answers. There is so much good that can come out of simply giving children a voice. Child Writes...

1. Promotes and improves literacy
2. Increases computer skills
3. Empowers children through discipline and contribution to others
4. Recognises children's abilities
5. Expands worldviews by making real world decisions
6. Creates reading opportunities for all students
7. Builds respectful communities by giving children a voice
8. Helps children in crisis
9. Provides commercial opportunities for budding authors

"A benefit of having Child Writes as part of the classroom instruction is its promotion of literacy. There is a noticeable increase in interest in literacy in our school since the introduction of the program."
Norah Murphy, Principal, Eidsvold State School

"Thank you for providing Lydia with this wonderful opportunity to create her own picture book. As a teacher and a parent at Middle Ridge, I have seen the results of the wonderful program that you so generously offer to the children at the school."
Susan Kath, Teacher and Parent

"I have been honoured to be a part of the Child Writes project from its second year, with both of my daughters participating in, and absolutely loving the process of writing and illustrating their own books. What an incredible experience - for everyone involved! Emma's patience and constant motivation ensured that both of these books came to a wonderful completion. For the girls to go to the State Library in Brisbane and be able to request a copy of their books from the Archive section was a huge thrill for all of us. Thank you Emma, for an experience most adults only dream about!"
Shana Rogers, Parent

Submit your request for further information at:
www.childwrites.com.au
Select 'Incorporate the Child Writes program into your school'

Get the Books!

child writes™

All books written and illustrated by children for children, as part of the Child Writes program, are available in the writers' web online bookstore.

www.writersweb.com.au

... connects writers direct to their reading audience
... allows emerging Australian writers to have their work read
... places the book directly into the hands of potential purchasers, the reader.

writers' web
where Australian writers become authors